C. S. LEWIS (1898–1963), an Oxford don and Cambridge professor, was the author of over twenty works, including the classic *Allegory of Love*, as well as *Mere Christianity*, several works of fantasy literature, and the children's work *The Lion, the Witch and the Wardrobe*. He was a member of the Oxford Christian group which included J. R. R. Tolkien and Charles Williams.

RICHARD GILMAN is the author of five books, including the spiritual autobiography *Faith, Sex, Mystery*.

𝒪

THE GREATS OF BRITAIN

The Screwtape Letters

BY

C. S. Lewis

with an Introduction by
Richard Gilman

A MENTOR BOOK

MENTOR
Published by the Penguin Group
Penguin Books USA Inc., 375 Hudson Street,
New York, New York 10014, U.S.A.
Penguin Books Ltd, 27 Wrights Lane,
London W8 5TZ, England
Penguin Books Australia Ltd, Ringwood,
Victoria, Australia
Penguin Books Canada Ltd, 10 Alcorn Avenue,
Toronto, Ontario, Canada M4V 3B2
Penguin Books (N.Z.) Ltd, 182–190 Wairau Road,
Auckland 10, New Zealand

Penguin Books Ltd, Registered Offices:
Harmondsworth, Middlesex, England

Published by Mentor, an imprint of New American Library,
a division of Penguin Books USA Inc.

First Mentor Printing, February, 1988
11 10 9 8 7 6 5 4 3

Introduction copyright © 1988 by Richard Gilman
All rights reserved

REGISTERED TRADEMARK—MARCA REGISTRADA

Library of Congress Catalog Card Number: 87-62468

Printed in the United States of America

Introduction

On July 20, 1940, during the first wartime summer in England, Clive Staples Lewis wrote to his brother Warren: "I [have been] struck by an idea for a book which I think might be useful and entertaining. It would be called 'As one Devil to another' and would consist of letters from an elderly retired devil to a young devil who has just started work on his first 'patient.' The idea would be to give all the psychology of temptation from the *other* point of view."

The next year the book was published under the title *The Screwtape Letters* and brought almost immediate fame to its author, a comparatively little-known forty-two-year-old writer and Oxford don whose fields of study were classical, medieval, renaissance, and early English literature. In 1943 the book was published in the United States, where it would prove to be Lewis's most widely read and influential work. Some years later an American biographer of Lewis, Chad Walsh, wrote that "here at last was a religious book, indeed a specifically Christian book, written with such sophistication and elegance that one need not apologize for leaving it out on the coffee table."

C. S. Lewis had been born in Belfast in 1898 into an upper-middle class Irish Protestant—though not especially pious—family; had become an avowed, not to say outspoken, atheist in his teens; and had undergone a conversion or "re-conversion" in his early thirties. A prolific writer, he would produce before his death in 1963 a diverse *oeuvre*, one that included volumes of poetry, erudite literary studies, science fiction, and a series of stories and novels for children, in addition of course to the religious and philosophical writings for which he was perhaps best known. Though he was an Anglican, his books of popular (some unfriendly critics would say "popularizing") theology and exposition of the Christian faith had a wide and enthusiastic Roman Catholic readership in England and, even more, in this country. I have an idea that my own encounter with his work was rather typical.

Actually, I wasn't a Catholic when I first read Lewis in the early nineteen fifties, but I was well on the way to becoming one, having passed through successive stages of nominal Judaism, aggressive atheism, and the beginning of an attraction toward the Church. It was a Jesuit priest in charge of a small lending library attached to St. Ignatius church in New York who introduced me to Lewis's writing.

I had gone into the library on an impulse and stayed for more than an hour discussing with the priest my interest in and difficulties with religion. When I left I was carrying an armful of books, among them Lewis's *Miracles*, *The Problem of*

Pain, and, if memory serves, *Beyond Christianity* ("He's not Catholic," the priest had told me, "but he's very highly regarded")—along with some novels by Graham Greene and François Mauriac as well as *The Everlasting Man* by G. K. Chesterton, who, I learned later, had been an important stylistic and thematic mentor of Lewis. (Some months after my baptism a year or so later I read *The Screwtape Letters* for the first time.)

What struck me at once about Lewis's accounts and exegeses of Christian belief and doctrine was the unemotional, rigorously (though not aridly) logical nature of his arguments. They were largely free of technical terminology or jargon and proceeded for the most part in a coolly reasonable fashion (at Oxford Lewis had a reputation as a most formidable debater) designed to win the reader's assent without either inflaming or alarming him. His methods resembled Chesterton's in some ways, as well as Bernard Shaw's in his dramatic prefaces and social commentary, making use of paradox, irony, and reversal as rhetorical instruments to throw unexpected light on what was conventionally opaque or denatured by familiarity.

Walter Hooper, an acolyte and later biographer of Lewis, said of him that "he has probably got more orthodox Christianity into more heads than any religious writer than . . . Chesterton." Lewis, however, thought of himself as more of a conduit than a proselytizer. "My task," he once wrote, "was . . . simply that of a *translator*—one turning Christian doctrine, or what he believed to be such, into the vernacular, into language that unscholarly people would attend to and could understand."

I wasn't entirely unscholarly at the time, but neither did I have any theological training or bent. Lewis's books therefore helped make Christianity available to me; in particular they served as a very useful antidote to the conventionally pious and intellectually flaccid spiritual writings through which I had been picking my way with distaste. One thing that much impressed me was his insistence that religion was no panacea, that it wouldn't automatically make a person "feel better." As he wrote in a 1946 essay called "Man or Rabbit?": ". . . foolish preachers, by always telling you how much Christianity will help you and how good it is for society, have actually led you to forget that Christianity is not a patent medicine."

But is there any doubt that Christianity is in fact widely regarded as a patent medicine in the United States today (are there televangelists in England?), hawked and peddled by an astonishing array of foolish preachers? Lewis wrote most of his spiritual books before the age of TV or before it had reached its full propagandistic power, but he would surely have addressed himself to both its blatancy and its insidiousness, refining or adapting his methods, maybe even going on the air as a counter-voice. For at the heart of his thinking and belief was the unaccommodating and unfashionable notion that one is or becomes religious not because of religion's usefulness but because of its truth. Get your patient to " 'believe this, not because it is true, but for some other reason,' that's the game," Screwtape tells his nephew.

Now the reader who picks up *The Screwtape Letters* for the first time will at once be faced with a central question: Is the book's underlying assumption itself true—which is to say is there really such a creature or being as the devil—or are we to regard the whole thing as a literary or philosophical conceit of Lewis's? Though Lewis never quoted it, Baudelaire's remark that "the devil's first wile is to convince us that he doesn't exist" comes to my mind. Well, at the risk of doing a certain injustice, or even violence, to Lewis's beliefs, I'll argue that one doesn't have to accept the reality of the devil to be able to respond more or less fully to the proposals and perceptions of *The Screwtape Letters*.

For whether or not the devil exists, Lewis's pertinent vision in the book is of temptations and proclivities toward evil, corruption, and vice that *do* exist, in us. Moreover, unlike the great majority of present-day evangelists and fundamentalist orators, for whom the devil is the direct cause and agent of evil (and so in effect a scapegoat, a creature that gets us off the hook), Lewis has a subtle and responsible sense of the matter. All the advice that the retired old demon Screwtape gives to his nephew, the novice Wormwood, rests on the assumption that human beings are the originators of their own evil and that the satanic function and task is that of keeping us on the downward path by promoting and encouraging in us confusion, rationalization, ignorance, and self-deception. In this light the devil may be thought of as the principle of our own blindness, a figure for our self-damnation.

In keeping with the book's sophisticated premise, its idea of how in this unbelieving age Hell or the underworld might operate, the devils of the correspondence are members of an elaborate enterprise organized along corporate or military lines, complete with "Training College," "Record Office," and "High Command." Beyond this, many of the tropes of faith are reversed; Screwtape speaks of the chief devil as "Our Father below" and "His Abysmal Sublimity" and refers to the "Lowerarchy" and the "Miserific Vision." Lewis isn't simply having verbal fun but pointing out how Hell is the *inversion* of Heaven, not a convenient melodramatic place where divinity dumps its human failures.

The originality of *The Screwtape Letters* begins with its presentation of the "other" point of view. By offering the devil's perspective on human folly and vice, Lewis infuses the book with a dramatic quality not ordinarily to be found in spiritual or moral treatises. (An obvious exception is *Pilgrim's Progress*, which Lewis greatly admired.) In addition to this, by concentrating on what we might call quotidian vices and temptations, unspectacular malfeasances, he is able to reveal the homely texture of our moral life—indeed to reveal the moral nature of qualities and actions we usually think of as lying outside ethics. We are far more likely to be "damned," however we interpret that, by our normal behavior than by extreme actions, major "sins." "The safest road to Hell," Screwtape tells Wormwood, meaning by safer the most assured way for the devils to gain their ends, "is the gradual one—the gentle slope, soft underfoot, without sudden turnings, without milestones, without signposts."

Screwtape's strategy for "undermining faith and preventing the formation of virtues" presupposes a target who is already technically religious or somewhat disposed toward it, and it is much more subtle and effective than a direct encouragement of vice would be. The great trick is to make us think we are virtuous when in fact we are not, and to this end the satanic plan makes use of many of those qualities we conventionally consider desirable: high-mindedness, good taste, appreciation of the new, etc.

The point once again is to get the "patient" to make decisions and choices not on the basis of truth but "for some other reason." "Don't waste time trying to make him think that materialism is *true*! Make him think it is strong, or stark, or courageous . . . the philosophy of the future." "Keep his mind off the most elementary duties by directing it to the most advanced and spiritual ones"; encourage in him "a vaguely devotional *mood* in which real concentration of will and intelligence has no part"; get him to "go all over the neighborhood looking for a church that 'suits' him until he becomes a taster and connoisseur of churches."

All this puts me in mind of that condition of morale and morality that has grown steadily more pervasive and entrenched since Lewis wrote.

Pragmatism in every area, self-indulgence as a right and even a duty, everything that's summed up in the formula: If it works or feels good, do it. *The Screwtape Letters* anticipates and warns against the blurring of the lines between the spiritual and the secular—the conversion, really, of the spiritual into its opposite.

Charles Peguy once defined the "bourgeois mind," by which he meant something beyond economic or social categories, as that which invariably "prefers the visible to the invisible." This of course is a major component of an antireligious or falsely religious attitude ("false spirituality is always to be encouraged," Screwtape says), as it is the source of the chief scandal of our age—religion as utility. "One of our best weapons is contented worldliness," Screwtape writes; and again, ". . . make men treat Christianity as a means, preferably, of course, as a means to their own advancement."

This anticipates Jerry Falwell's assertion that "wealth is God's way of rewarding those who put Him first" and his injunction to "put Jesus first in your stewardship and allow Him to bless you financially," just as it foreshadows Jim Bakker's and Oral Roberts's turning of religion into a growth stock. But the phenomenon has far older roots in religious history, both Catholic and Protestant, and, to be sure, in human nature itself. Screwtape urges Wormwood to exacerbate in his patient an itch for possession—". . . the sense of ownership . . . is always to be encouraged"—and to press toward the atomization of society through selfish competition. In one of the central statements of the "other" viewpoint he writes: "The whole philosophy of Hell rests on recognition of the axiom that one thing is not another thing, and, specially, that one self is not another self. My good is my good and your good is yours. What one gains the other loses."

This view of the world as competition, of life as profit and loss, power and defeat, is a profound inversion of the Christian ethic and of religion's basis in loving communality. And it is what so largely reigns in our time. But while the self will surely be lost through solipsism, an insistence on one's "rights" and well-being at the expense of others—at the expense, therefore, of love and altruism—it can also be lost by ceding its genuineness and truth. "It is always desirable," Screwtape tells Wormwood, "to substitute the standards of the World, or convention, or fashion, for a human's real likings and dislikings. . . . You should always try to make the patient abandon the people or food or books he really likes in favour of the 'best' people, the 'right' food, the 'important' books."

And still another way to create inauthentic life is to make our minds dwell on the future: ". . . in making them think about [it] we make them think of unrealities . . . we want a man hag-ridden by the Future—haunted by visions of an imminent heaven or hell upon earth . . . we want a whole race perpetually in pursuit of the rainbow's end, never honest, nor kind, nor happy *now*." Nothing better indicates the *Letters'* originality as moral inquiry than this shrewd observation about the way we escape the struggles and responsibilities of actual life by residing in one that doesn't yet exist.

For the most part the Christian point of view is revealed by implication from Screwtape's injunctions and advice: If, for example, he urges Wormwood to encourage our selfishness, then generosity is the virtue in question. But there are occasions in the book when Lewis speaks directly about goodness and faith, utterances that are wrested reluctantly, as it were, from the old devil. "The most repellant and inexplicable trait in our Enemy," he says, "[is that] He *really* loves the hairless bipeds He has created." Again, in speaking of our belief in the power and self-sufficiency of romantic love he says that it "is not enough . . . charity is needed." At the same time he warns his nephew not to trust too much in the usefulness of sexual acts as instruments for damnation, remarking on "those generous and imaginative and even spiritual concomitants which often render human sexuality so disappointing."

I suspect that passages such as these, along with others in which Lewis gives answers—always through Screwtape, of course—to perennial problems like free will or the nature of spiritual humility, afforded him relief from the exhausting and, in a certain sense, distasteful task he'd set himself. *The Screwtape Letters*, he once told an interviewer, was the only book that "I did not take pleasure in writing. At the time, I was thinking of objections to the Christian life, and decided to put them into the form, 'That's what the devil would say.' But making goods 'bad' and bads 'good' gets to be fatiguing." Another time he wrote: "The world into which I had to project myself while I spoke through Screwtape was all dust, grit, thirst and itch. Every trace of beauty, freshness and geniality had to be excluded. It almost smothered me before I was done."

But it didn't. Nor was he able to exclude beauty and freshness, as he thought he had. I think of his lovely lines about music and silence, our only weapons against the unbearable *noise* of the world, and of his remark about laughter being a "direct insult to the realism . . . and austerity of Hell." Lewis may have had to enter the world of a devil, but he infused it, against the creature's will, naturally, with geniality and wit. In their biography of Lewis, Roger Green and Walter Hooper tell the story of a "country clergyman who . . . wrote to the editor [of *The Guardian*, where *The Screwtape Letters* had appeared serially] canceling his subscription on the ground that 'much of the advice given in these letters seemed to him not only erroneous but positively diabolic.' " Lewis is reported to have roared with delight; he could not have asked for a better proof of the book's triumphant strategy.

—RICHARD GILMAN

to J. R. R. Tolkien

Preface

I have no intention of explaining how the correspondence which I now offer to the public fell into my hands.

There are two equal and opposite errors into which our race can fall about the devils. One is to disbelieve in their existence. The other is to believe, and to feel an excessive and unhealthy interest in them. They themselves are equally pleased by both errors, and hail a materialist or a magician with the same delight. The sort of script which is used in this book can be very easily obtained by anyone who has once learned the knack; but ill-disposed or excitable people who might make a bad use of it shall not learn it from me.

Readers are advised to remember that the devil is a liar. Not everything that Screwtape says should be assumed to be true even from his own angle. I have made no attempt to identify any of the human beings mentioned in the letters; but I think it very unlikely that the portraits, say, of Fr. Spike or the patient's mother, are wholly just. There is wishful thinking in Hell as well as on Earth.

In conclusion, I ought to add that no effect has been made to clear up the chronology of the letters. Number XVII appears to have been composed before rationing became serious; but in general the diabolical method of dating seems to bear no relation to terrestrial time, and I have not attempted to reproduce it. The history of the European War, except in so far as it happens now and then to impinge upon the spiritual condition of one human being, was obviously of no interest to Screwtape.

C. S. LEWIS

Magdalen College
July 5, 1941

"The best way to drive out the devil, if he will not yield to texts of Scripture, is to jeer and flout him, for he cannot bear scorn."

—Luther

———

"The devil . . . the prowde spirite . . . cannot endure to be mocked."

—Thomas More

*M*y dear Wormwood,

I note what you say about guiding your patient's reading and taking care that he sees a good deal of his materialist friend. But are you not being a trifle *naïf*? It sounds as if you supposed that *argument* was the way to keep him out of the Enemy's clutches. That might have been so if he had lived a few centuries earlier. At that time the humans still knew pretty well when a thing was proved and when it was not; and if it was proved they really believed it. They still connected thinking with doing and were prepared to alter their way of life as the result of a chain of reasoning. But what with the weekly press and other such weapons we have largely altered that. Your man has been accustomed, ever since he was a boy, to have a dozen incompatible philosophies dancing about together inside his head. He doesn't think of doctrines as primarily "true" or "false," but as "academic" or "practical," "outworn" or "contemporary," "conventional" or "ruthless." Jargon, not argument, is your best ally in keeping him from the Church. Don't waste time trying to make him

1

think that materialism is *true!* Make him think it is strong, or stark, or courageous—that it is the philosophy of the future. That's the sort of thing he cares about.

The trouble about argument is that it moves the whole struggle onto the Enemy's own ground. He can argue too; whereas in really practical propaganda of the kind I am suggesting He has been shown for centuries to be greatly the inferior of Our Father Below. By the very act of arguing, you awake the patient's reason; and once it is awake, who can foresee the result? Even if a particular train of thought can be twisted so as to end in our favour, you will find that you have been strengthening in your patient the fatal habit of attending to universal issues and withdrawing his attention from the stream of immediate sense experiences. Your business is to fix his attention on the stream. Teach him to call it "real life" and don't let him ask what he means by "real."

Remember, he is not, like you, a pure spirit. Never having been a human (oh, that abominable advantage of the Enemy's!) you don't realise how enslaved they are to the pressure of the ordinary. I once had a patient, a sound atheist, who used to read in the British Museum. One day, as he sat reading, I saw a train of thought in his mind beginning to go the wrong way. The Enemy, of course, was at his elbow in a moment. Before I knew where I was I saw my twenty years' work beginning to totter. If I had lost my head and begun to attempt a defence by argument, I should have been undone. But I was not such a fool. I struck instantly at the part of the man which I had best under my control, and suggested that it was just about time he had some lunch. The Enemy presumably made the counter-suggestion (you know how one can never *quite* overhear what He says to them?) that this was more important than lunch. At least I think that must have been His line, for when I said, "Quite. In fact much *too* important to tackle at the end of a morning," the patient brightened up considerably; and by the time I had added "Much better come back after lunch and go into it with a fresh mind," he was already halfway to the door. Once he was in the street the battle was won. I showed him a newsboy shouting the midday paper, and a No. 73 bus going past, and before he reached the bottom of the steps I had got into him an unalterable conviction that, whatever odd ideas might come into a man's head when he was shut up alone with his books, a healthy dose of "real life" (by which he meant the bus and the newsboy) was enough to show him that all "that sort of thing" just couldn't be true. He knew he'd had a narrow escape, and in later years was fond of talking about "that inarticulate sense for actuality which is our ultimate safeguard against the aberrations of mere logic." He is now safe in Our Father's house.

You begin to see the point? Thanks to processes which we set at work in them centuries ago, they find it all but impossible to believe in the unfamiliar while the familiar is before their eyes. Keep pressing home on him the *ordinariness* of things. Above all, do not attempt to use science

(I mean, the real sciences) as a defence against Christianity. They will positively encourage him to think about realities he can't touch and see. There have been sad cases among the modern physicists. If he must dabble in science, keep him on economics and sociology; don't let him get away from that invaluable "real life." But the best of all is to let him read no science but to give him a grand general idea that he knows it all and that everything he happens to have picked up in casual talk and reading is "the results of modern investigation." Do remember you are there to fuddle him. From the way some of you young fiends talk, anyone would suppose it was our job to *teach!*

Your affectionate uncle

SCREWTAPE

II

*M*y dear Wormwood,

I note with grave displeasure that your patient has become a Christian. Do not indulge the hope that you will escape the usual penalties; indeed, in your better moments, I trust you would hardly even wish to do so. In the meantime we must make the best of the situation. There is no need to despair; hundreds of these adult converts have been reclaimed after a brief sojourn in the Enemy's camp and are now with us. All the *habits* of the patient, both mental and bodily, are still in our favour.

One of our great allies at present is the Church itself. Do not misunderstand me. I do not mean the Church as we see her spread out through all time and space and rooted in eternity, terrible as an army with banners. That, I confess, is a spectacle which makes our boldest tempters uneasy. But fortunately it is quite invisible to these humans. All your patient sees is the half-finished, sham Gothic erection on the new building estate. When he goes inside, he sees the local grocer with rather an oily expression on his face bustling up to offer him one shiny little book containing a liturgy which neither of them understands, and one shabby little book containing corrupt texts of a number of religious lyrics, mostly bad, and in very small print. When he gets to his pew and looks round him he sees just that selection of his neighbours whom he has hitherto avoided. You want to lean pretty heavily on those neighbours. Make his mind flit to and fro between an expression like "the body of Christ" and the actual faces in the next pew. It matters very little, of course, what kind of people that next pew really contains. You may know one of them to be a great warrior on the Enemy's side. No matter. Your patient, thanks to Our Father Below, is a fool. Provided that any of those neighbours sing out of tune, or have boots that squeak, or double chins, or odd clothes, the patient will quite easily believe that their religion must therefore be somehow ridiculous. At his present stage, you see, he has an idea of "Christians" in his mind which he supposes to be spiritual but which, in fact, is largely pictorial. His mind is full of togas and sandals and armour and bare legs and the mere fact that the other people in church wear modern clothes is a real— though of course an unconscious—difficulty to him. Never let it come to the surface; never let him ask what he expected them to look like. Keep everything hazy in his mind now, and you will have all eternity wherein to amuse yourself by producing in him the peculiar kind of clarity which Hell affords.

Work hard, then, on the disappointment or an-

Free will.

ticlimax which is certainly coming to the patient during his first few weeks as a churchman. The Enemy allows this disappointment to occur on the threshold of every human endeavour. It occurs when the boy who has been enchanted in the nursery by *Stories from the Odyssey* buckles down to really learning Greek. It occurs when lovers have got married and begin the real task of learning to live together. In every department of life it marks the transition from dreaming aspiration to laborious doing. The Enemy takes this risk because He has a curious fantasy of making all these disgusting little human vermin into what He calls His "free" lovers and servants—"sons" is the word He uses, with His inveterate love of degrading the whole spiritual world by unnatural liaisons with the two-legged animals. Desiring their freedom, He therefore refuses to carry them, by their mere affections and habits, to any of the goals which He sets before them: He leaves them to "do it on their own." And there lies our opportunity. But also, remember, there lies our danger. If once they get through this initial dryness successfully, they become much less dependent on emotion and therefore much harder to tempt.

I have been writing hitherto on the assumption that the people in the next pew afford no *rational* ground for disappointment. Of course, if they do—if the patient knows that the woman with the absurd hat is a fanatical bridgeplayer or the man with squeaky boots a miser and an extortioner— then your task is so much the easier. All you then have to do is to keep out of his mind the question

"If I, being what I am, can consider that I am in some sense a Christian, why should the different vices of those people in the next pew prove that their religion is mere hypocrisy and convention?" You may ask whether it is possible to keep such an obvious thought from occurring even to a human mind. It is, Wormwood, it is! Handle him properly and it simply won't come into his head. He has not been anything like long enough with the Enemy to have any real humility yet. What he says, even on his knees, about his own sinfulness is all parrot talk. At bottom, he still believes he has run up a very favourable credit balance in the Enemy's ledger by allowing himself to be converted, and thinks that he is showing great humility and condescension in going to church with these "smug," commonplace neighbours at all. Keep him in that state of mind as long as you can.

Your affectionate uncle

SCREWTAPE

III

My dear Wormwood,

I am very pleased by what you tell me about this man's relations with his mother. But you must press your advantage. The Enemy will be working from the centre outwards, gradually bringing more and more of the patient's conduct under the new standard, and may reach his behaviour to the old lady at any moment. You want to get in first. Keep in close touch with our colleague Glubose who is in charge of the mother, and build up between you in that house a good settled habit of mutual annoyance: daily pinpricks. The following methods are useful.

1. Keep his mind on the inner life. He thinks his conversion is something *inside* him and his attention is therefore chiefly turned at present to the states of his own mind—or rather to that very expurgated version of them which is all you should allow him to see. Encourage this. Keep his mind off the most elementary duties by directing it to the most advanced and spiritual ones. Aggravate that most useful human characteristic, the horror and neglect of the obvious. You must bring

him to a condition in which he can practise self-examination for an hour without discovering any of those facts about himself which are perfectly clear to anyone who has ever lived in the same house with him or worked in the same office.

2. It is, no doubt, impossible to prevent his praying for his mother, but we have means of rendering the prayers innocuous. Make sure that they are always very "spiritual," that he is always concerned with the state of her soul and never with her rheumatism. Two advantages will follow. In the first place, his attention will be kept on what he regards as her sins, by which, with a little guidance from you, he can be induced to mean any of her actions which are inconvenient or irritating to himself. Thus you can keep rubbing the wounds of the day a little sorer even while he is on his knees; the operation is not at all difficult and you will find it very entertaining. In the second place, since his ideas about her soul will be very crude and often erroneous, he will, in some degree, be praying for an imaginary person, and it will be your task to make that imaginary person daily less and less like the real mother—the sharp-tongued old lady at the breakfast table. In time, you may get the cleavage so wide that no thought or feeling from his prayers for the imagined mother will ever flow over into his treatment of the real one. I have had patients of my own so well in hand that they could be turned at a moment's notice from impassioned prayer for a wife's or son's "soul" to beating or insulting the real wife or son without a qualm.

3. When two humans have lived together for many years, it usually happens that each has tones of voice and expressions of face which are almost unendurably irritating to the other. Work on that. Bring fully into the consciousness of your patient that particular lift of his mother's eyebrows which he learned to dislike in the nursery, and let him think how much he dislikes it. Let him assume that she knows how annoying it is and does it to annoy—if you know your job he will not notice the immense improbability of the assumption. And, of course, never let him suspect that he has tones and looks which similarly annoy her. As he cannot see or hear himself, this is easily managed.

4. In civilised life domestic hatred usually expresses itself by saying things which would appear quite harmless on paper (the *words* are not offensive) but in such a voice, or at such a moment, that they are not far short of a blow in the face. To keep this game up you and Glubose must see to it that each of these two fools has a sort of double standard. Your patient must demand that all his own utterances are to be taken at their face value and judged simply on the actual words, while at the same time judging all his mother's utterances with the fullest and most oversensitive interpretation of the tone and the context and the suspected intention. She must be encouraged to do the same to him. Hence from every quarrel they can both go away convinced, or very nearly convinced, that they are quite innocent. You know the kind of thing: "I simply ask her what time dinner will be and she flies into a temper." Once

this habit is well established you have the delightful situation of a human saying things with the express purpose of offending and yet having a grievance when offence is taken.

Finally, tell me something about the old lady's religious position. Is she at all jealous of the new factor in her son's life?—at all piqued that he should have learned from others, and so late, what she considers she gave him such good opportunity of learning in childhood? Does she feel he is making a great deal of "fuss" about it—or that he's getting in on very easy terms? Remember the elder brother in the Enemy's story.

Your affectionate uncle
SCREWTAPE

IV

*M*y dear Wormwood,

The amateurish suggestions in your last letter warn me that it is high time for me to write to you fully on the painful subject of prayer. You might have spared the comment that my advice about his prayers for his mother "proved singularly unfortunate." That is not the sort of thing that a nephew should write to his uncle—nor a junior tempter to the undersecretary of a department. It also reveals an unpleasant desire to shift responsibility; you must learn to pay for your own blunders.

The best thing, where it is possible, is to keep the patient from the serious intention of praying altogether. When the patient is an adult recently reconverted to the Enemy's party, like your man, this is best done by encouraging him to remember, or to think he remembers, the parrotlike nature of his prayers in childhood. In reaction against that, he may be persuaded to aim at something entirely spontaneous, inward, informal, and unregularised; and what this will actually mean to a beginner will be an effort to produce in him-

self a vaguely devotional mood in which real concentration of will and intelligence have no part.
One of their poets, Coleridge, has recorded that
he did not pray "with moving lips and bended
knees" but merely "composed his spirit to love"
and indulged "a sense of supplication." That is
exactly the sort of prayer we want; and since it
bears a superficial resemblance to the prayer of
silence as practised by those who are very far
advanced in the Enemy's service, clever and lazy
patients can be taken in by it for quite a long
time. At the very least, they can be persuaded that
the bodily position makes no difference to their
prayers; for they constantly forget, what you must
always remember, that they are animals and that
whatever their bodies do affects their souls. It is
funny how mortals always picture us as putting
things into their minds: in reality our best work
is done by keeping things out.

If this fails, you must fall back on a subtler
misdirection of his intention. Whenever they are
attending to the Enemy Himself we are defeated,
but there are ways of preventing them from doing
so. The simplest is to turn their gaze away from
Him towards themselves. Keep them watching their
own minds and trying to produce *feelings* there
by the action of their own wills. When they meant
to ask Him for charity, let them, instead, start
trying to manufacture charitable feelings for themselves and not notice that this is what they are
doing. When they meant to pray for courage, let
them really be trying to feel brave. When they say
they are praying for forgiveness, let them be trying

to feel forgiven. Teach them to estimate the value of each prayer by their success in producing the desired feeling; and never let them suspect how much success or failure of that kind depends on whether they are well or ill, fresh or tired, at the moment.

But of course the Enemy will not meantime be idle. Wherever there is prayer, there is danger of His own immediate action. He is cynically indifferent to the dignity of His position, and ours, as pure spirits, and to human animals on their knees He pours out self-knowledge in a quite shameless fashion. But even if He defeats your first attempt at misdirection, we have a subtler weapon. The humans do not start from that direct perception of Him which we, unhappily, cannot avoid. They have never known that ghastly luminosity, that stabbing and searing glare which makes the background of permanent pain to our lives. If you look into your patient's mind when he is praying, you will not find *that*. If you examine the object to which he is attending, you will find that it is a composite object containing many quite ridiculous ingredients. There will be images derived from pictures of the Enemy as He appeared during the discreditable episode known as the Incarnation: there will be vaguer—perhaps quite savage and puerile—images associated with the other two Persons. There will even be some of his own reverence (and of bodily sensations accompanying it) objectified and attributed to the object revered. I have known cases where what the patient called his "God" was actually *located*—up and to the left at the corner of the bedroom ceiling, or inside his own head, or in a crucifix on the wall. But whatever the nature of the composite object, you must keep him praying to *it*—to the thing that he has made, not to the Person who has made him. You may even encourage him to attach great importance to the correction and improvement of his composite object, and to keeping it steadily before his imagination during the whole prayer. For if he ever comes to make the distinction, if ever he consciously directs his prayers "Not to what I think thou art but to what thou knowest thyself to be," our situation is, for the moment, desperate. Once all his thoughts and images have been flung aside or, if retained, retained with a full recognition of their merely subjective nature, and the man trusts himself to the completely real, external, invisible Presence, there with him in the room and never knowable by him as he is known by it—why, then it is that the incalculable may occur. In avoiding this situation—this real nakedness of the soul in prayer—you will be helped by the fact that the humans themselves do not desire it as much as they suppose. There's such a thing as getting more than they bargained for!

Your affectionate uncle

SCREWTAPE

V

*M*y dear Wormwood,

It is a little bit disappointing to expect a detailed report on your work and to receive instead such a vague rhapsody as your last letter. You say you are "delirious with joy" because the European humans have started another of their wars. I see very well what has happened to you. You are not delirious; you are only drunk. Reading between the lines in your very unbalanced account of the patient's sleepless night, I can reconstruct your state of mind fairly accurately. For the first time in your career you have tasted that wine which is the reward of all our labours—the anguish and bewilderment of a human soul—and it has gone to your head. I can hardly blame you. I do not expect old heads on young shoulders. Did the patient respond to some of your terror-pictures of the future? Did you work in some good self-pitying glances at the happy past?—some fine thrills in the pit of his stomach, were there? You played your violin prettily, did you? Well, well, it's all very natural. But do remember, Wormwood, that duty comes before pleasure. If any present self-indulgence on your part leads to the ultimate loss of the prey, you will be left eternally thirsting for that draught of which you are now so much enjoying your first sip. If, on the other hand, by steady and cool-headed application here and now you can finally secure his soul, he will then be yours forever—a brimfull living chalice of despair and horror and astonishment which you can raise to your lips as often as you please. So do not allow any temporary excitement to distract you from the real business of undermining faith and preventing the formation of virtues. Give me without fail in your next letter a full account of the patient's reactions to the war, so that we can consider whether you are likely to do more good by making him an extreme patriot or an ardent pacifist. There are all sorts of possibilities. In the meantime, I must warn you not to hope too much from a war.

Of course a war is entertaining. The immediate fear and suffering of the humans is a legitimate and pleasing refreshment for our myriads of toiling workers. But what permanent good does it do us unless we make use of it for bringing souls to Our Father Below? When I see the temporal suffering of humans who finally escape us, I feel as if I had been allowed to taste the first course of a rich banquet and then denied the rest. It is worse than not to have tasted it at all. The Enemy, true to His barbarous methods of warfare, allows us to see the short misery of His favourites only to tantalise and torment us—to mock the incessant hunger which, during this present phase of the great conflict, His blockade is admittedly imposing. Let us therefore think rather how to use, than how to enjoy, this European war. For it has certain tendencies inherent in it which are, in themselves, by no means in our favour. We may hope for a good deal of cruelty and unchastity. But, if we are not careful, we shall see thousands turning in this tribulation to the Enemy, while tens of thousands who do not go so far as that will nevertheless have their attention diverted from themselves to values and causes which they believe to be higher than the self. I know that the Enemy disapproves many of these causes. But that is where He is so unfair. He often makes prizes of humans who have given their lives for causes He thinks bad on the monstrously sophistical ground that the humans thought them good and were following the best they knew. Consider too what undesirable deaths occur in wartime. Men are killed in places where they knew they might be killed and to which they go, if they are at all of the Enemy's party prepared. How much better for us if *all* humans died in costly nursing homes amid doctors who lie, nurses who lie, friends who lie, as we have trained them, promising life to the dying, encouraging the belief that sickness excuses every indulgence, and even, if our workers know their job, withholding all suggestion of a priest lest it should betray to the sick man his true condition! And how disastrous for us is the continual remembrance of death which war enforces. One of our best weapons, contented worldliness, is rendered useless. In wartime not even a human can believe that he is going to live forever.

I know that Scabtree and others have seen in wars a great opportunity for attacks on faith, but I think that view was exaggerated. The Enemy's human partisans have all been plainly told by Him that suffering is an essential part of what He calls Redemption; so that a faith which is destroyed by a war or a pestilence cannot really have been worth the trouble of destroying. I am speaking now of diffused suffering over a long period such as the war will produce. Of course, at the precise moment of terror, bereavement, or physical pain, you may catch your man when his reason is temporarily suspended. But even then, if he applies to Enemy headquarters, I have found that the post is nearly always defended.

Your affectionate uncle
SCREWTAPE

VI

My dear Wormwood,

I am delighted to hear that your patient's age and profession make it possible, but by no means certain, that he will be called up for military service. We want him to be in the maximum uncertainty, so that his mind will be filled with contradictory pictures of the future, every one of which arouses hope or fear. There is nothing like suspense and anxiety for barricading a human's mind against the Enemy. He wants men to be concerned with what they do; our business is to keep them thinking about what will happen to them.

Your patient will, of course, have picked up the notion that he must submit with patience to the Enemy's will. What the Enemy means by this is primarily that he should accept with patience the tribulation which has actually been dealt out to him—the present anxiety and suspense. It is about *this* that he is to say "Thy will be done," and for the daily task of bearing *this* that the daily bread will be provided. It is your business to see that the patient never thinks of the present fear as his appointed cross, but only of the things he is afraid of. Let him regard them as his crosses: let him forget that, since they are incompatible, they cannot all happen to him, and let him try to practise fortitude and patience to them all in advance. For real resignation, at the same moment, to a dozen different and hypothetical fates, is almost impossible, and the Enemy does not greatly assist those who are trying to attain it: resignation to present and actual suffering, even where that suffering consists of fear, is far easier, and is usually helped by this direct action. *Anxiety doesn't help anything*

An important spiritual law is here involved. I have explained that you can weaken his prayers by diverting his attention from the Enemy Himself to his own states of mind about the Enemy. On the other hand fear becomes easier to master when the patient's mind is diverted from the thing feared to the fear itself, considered as a present and undesirable state of his own mind; and when he regards the fear as his appointed cross he will inevitably think of it as a state of mind. One can therefore formulate the general rule: In all activities of mind which favour our cause, encourage the patient to be un-selfconscious and to concentrate on the object, but in all activities favourable to the Enemy bend his mind back on itself. Let an insult or a woman's body so fix his attention outward that he does not reflect "I am now entering into the state called Anger—or the state called Lust." Contrariwise let the reflection "My feelings are now growing more devout, or more charitable," so fix his attention inward that he no longer looks beyond himself to see our Enemy or his own neighbours.

As regards his more general attitude to the war, you must not rely too much on those feelings of hatred which the humans are so fond of discussing in Christian, or anti-Christian, periodicals. In his anguish, the patient can, of course, be encouraged to revenge himself by some vindictive feelings directed towards the German leaders, and that is good so far as it goes. But it is usually a sort of melodramatic or mythical hatred directed against imaginary scapegoats. He has never met these people in real life—they are lay figures modelled on what he gets from newspapers. The results of such fanciful hatred are often most disappointing and of all humans the English are in this respect the most deplorable milksops. They are creatures of that miserable sort who loudly proclaim that torture is too good for their enemies and then give tea and cigarettes to the first wounded German pilot who turns up at the back door.

Do what you will, there is going to be some benevolence, as well as some malice, in your patient's soul. The great thing is to direct the malice to his immediate neighbours whom he meets every day and to thrust his benvolence out to the remote circumference, to people he does not know. The malice thus becomes wholly real and the benevolence largely imaginary. There is no good at all in inflaming his hatred of Germans if, at the same time, a pernicious habit of charity is growing up between him and his mother, his em-

shoves virtue outward + hatred inward

ployer, and the man he meets in the train. Think of your man as a series of concentric circles, his will being the innermost, his intellect coming next, and finally his fantasy. You can hardly hope, at once, to exclude from all the circles everything that smells of the Enemy: but you must keep on shoving all the virtues outward till they are finally located in the circle of fantasy, and all the desirable qualities inward into the Will. It is only in so far as they reach the will and are there embodied in habits that the virtues are really fatal to us. (I don't, of course, mean what the patient mistakes for his will, the conscious fume and fret of resolutions and clenched teeth, but the real centre, what the Enemy calls the Heart.) All sorts of virtues painted in the fantasy or approved by the intellect or even, in some measure, loved and admired, will not keep a man from Our Father's house: indeed they may make him more amusing when he gets there.

Your affectionate uncle

SCREWTAPE

VII

*M*y dear Wormwood,

I wonder you should ask me whether it is essential to keep the patient in ignorance of your own existence. That question, at least for the present phase of the struggle, has been answered for us by the High Command. Our policy, for the moment, is to conceal ourselves. Of course this has not always been so. We are really faced with a cruel dilemma. When the humans disbelieve in our existence we lose all the pleasing results of direct terrorism and we make no magicians. On the other hand, when they believe in us, we cannot make them materialists and sceptics. At least, not yet. I have great hopes that we shall learn in due time how to emotionalise and mythologise their science to such an extent that what is, in effect, a belief in us (though not under that name) will creep in while the human mind remains closed to belief in the Enemy. The "Life Force," the worship of sex, and some aspects of Psychoanalysis may here prove useful. If once we can produce our perfect work—the Materialist Magician, the man, not using, but veritably worshipping, what he

25

vaguely calls "Forces" while denying the existence of "spirits"—then the end of the war will be in sight. But in the meantime we must obey our orders. I do not think you will have much difficulty in keeping the patient in the dark. The fact that "devils" are predominantly *comic* figures in the modern imagination will help you. If any faint suspicion of your existence begins to arise in his mind, suggest to him a picture of something in red tights, and persuade him that since he cannot believe in that (it is an old textbook method of confusing them) he therefore cannot believe in you.

I had not forgotten my promise to consider whether we should make the patient an extreme patriot or an extreme pacifist. All extremes except extreme devotion to the Enemy are to be encouraged. Not always, of course, but at this period. Some ages are lukewarm and complacent, and then it is our business to soothe them yet faster asleep. Other ages, of which the present is one, are unbalanced and prone to faction, and it is our business to inflame them. Any small coterie, bound together by some interest which other men dislike or ignore, tends to develop inside itself a hothouse mutual admiration, and towards the outer world, a great deal of pride and hatred which is entertained without shame because the "Cause" is its sponsor and it is thought to be impersonal. Even when the little group exists originally for the Enemy's own purposes, this remains true. We want the Church to be small not only that fewer men may know the Enemy but also that those who do may acquire the uneasy intensity and the defensive self-righteousness of a secret society or a clique. The Church herself is, of course, heavily defended and we have never yet quite succeeded in giving her *all* the characteristics of a faction; but subordinate factions within her have often produced admirable results, from the parties of Paul and of Apollos at Corinth down to the High and Low parties in the Church of England.

If your patient can be induced to become a conscientious objector he will automatically find himself one of a small, vocal, organised, and unpopular society, and the effects of this, on one so new to Christianity, will almost certainly be good. But only *almost* certainly. Has he had serious doubts about the lawfulness of serving in a just war before this present war began? Is he a man of great physical courage—so great that he will have no half-conscious misgivings about the real motives of his pacifism? Can he, when nearest to honesty (no human is ever *very* near), feel fully convinced that he is actuated wholly by the desire to obey the Enemy? If he is that sort of man, his pacifism will probably not do us much good, and the Enemy will probably protect him from the usual consequences of belonging to a sect. Your best plan, in that case, would be to attempt a sudden, confused, emotional crisis from which he might emerge as an uneasy convert to patriotism. Such things can often be managed. But if he is the man I take him to be, try Pacifism.

Whichever he adopts, your main task will be the

same. Let him begin by treating the Patriotism or the Pacifism as a part of his religion. Then let him, under the influence of partisan spirit, come to regard it as the most important part. Then quietly and gradually nurse him on to the stage at which the religion becomes merely part of the "Cause," in which Christianity is valued chiefly because of the excellent arguments it can produce in favour of the British war effort or of pacifism. The attitude which you want to guard against is that in which temporal affairs are treated primarily as material for obedience. Once you have made the World an end, and faith a means, you have almost won your man, and it makes very little difference what kind of worldly end he is pursuing. Provided that meetings, pamphlets, policies, movements, causes, and crusades, matter more to him than prayers and sacraments and charity, he is ours—and the more "religious" (on those terms), the more securely ours. I could show you a pretty cageful down here.

Your affectionate uncle
SCREWTAPE

VIII

peaks + valleys

*M*y dear Wormwood,

So you "have great hopes that the patient's religious phase is dying away," have you? I always thought the Training College had gone to pieces since they put old Slubgob at the head of it, and now I am sure. Has no one ever told you about the law of Undulation?

Humans are amphibians—half spirit and half animal. (The Enemy's determination to produce such a revolting hybrid was one of the things that determined Our Father to withdraw his support from Him.) As spirits they belong to the eternal world, but as animals they inhabit time. This means that while their spirit can be directed to an eternal object, their bodies, passions, and imaginations are in continual change, for to be in time means to change. Their nearest approach to constancy, therefore, is undulation—the repeated return to a level from which they repeatedly fall back, a series of troughs and peaks. If you had watched your patient carefully you would have seen this undulation in every department of his life—his interest in his work, his affection for his friends, his physical appetites, all go up and down. As long as he lives on earth, periods of emotional and bodily richness and liveliness will alternate with periods of numbness and poverty. The dryness and dullness through which your patient is now going are not, as you fondly suppose, your workmanship; they are merely a natural phenomenon which will do us no good unless you make a good use of it.

To decide what the best use of it is, you must ask what use the Enemy wants to make of it, and then do the opposite. Now, it may surprise you to learn that in His efforts to get permanent possession of a soul, He relies on the troughs even more than on the peaks; some of His special favourites have gone through longer and deeper troughs than anyone else. The reason is this. To us a human is primarily food; our aim is the absorption of its will into ours, the increase of our own area of selfhood at its expense. But the obedience which the Enemy demands of men is quite a different thing. One must face the fact that all the talk about His love for men, and His service being perfect freedom, is not (as one would gladly believe) mere propaganda, but an appalling truth. He really *does* want to fill the universe with a lot of loathsome little replicas of Himself—creatures whose life, on its miniature scale, will be qualitatively like His own, not because He has absorbed them but because their wills freely conform to His. We want cattle who can finally become food; He wants servants who can finally become sons. We want to suck in, He wants to give out. We are empty and would be filled; He is full and flows over. Our war aim is a world in which Our Father Below has drawn all other beings into himself: the Enemy wants a world full of beings united to Him but still distinct.

And that is where the troughs come in. You must have often wondered why the Enemy does not make more use of His power to be sensibly present to human souls in any degree He chooses and at any moment. But you now see that the Irresistible and the Indisputable are the two weapons which the very nature of His scheme forbids Him to use. Merely to override a human will (as His felt presence in any but the faintest and most mitigated degree would certainly do) would be for Him useless. He cannot ravish. He can only woo. For His ignoble idea is to eat the cake and have it; the creatures are to be one with Him, but yet themselves; merely to cancel them, or assimilate them, will not serve. He is prepared to do a little overriding at the beginning. He will set them off with communications of His presence which, though faint, seem great to them, with emotional sweetness, and easy conquest over temptation. But He never allows this state of affairs to last long. Sooner or later He withdraws, if not in fact, at least from their conscious experience, all those supports and incentives. He leaves the creature to stand up on its own legs—to carry out from the will alone duties which have lost all relish. It is during such trough periods, much more than during the peak periods, that it is growing into the sort of creature He wants it to be. Hence the prayers offered in the state of dryness are those which please Him best. We can drag our patients along by continual tempting, because we design them only for the table, and the more their will is interfered with the better. He cannot "tempt" to virtue as we do to vice. He wants them to learn to walk and must therefore take away His hand; and if only the will to walk is really there He is pleased even with their stumbles. Do not be deceived, Wormwood. Our cause is never more in danger than when a human, no longer desiring, but still intending, to do our Enemy's will, looks round upon a universe from which every trace of Him seems to have vanished, and asks why he has been forsaken, and still obeys.

But of course the troughs afford opportunities to our side also. Next week I will give you some hints on how to exploit them.

Your affectionate uncle

SCREWTAPE

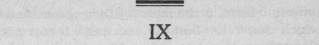

IX

My dear Wormwood,

I hope my last letter has convinced you that the trough of dullness or "dryness" through which your patient is going at present will not, of itself, give you his soul, but needs to be properly exploited. What forms the exploitation should take I shall now consider.

In the first place I have always found that the Trough periods of the human undulation provide excellent opportunity for all sensual temptations, particularly those of sex. This may surprise you, because, of course, there is more physical energy, and therefore more potential appetite, at the Peak periods; but you must remember that the powers of resistance are then also at their highest. The health and spirits which you want to use in producing lust can also, alas, be very easily used for work or play or thought or innocuous merriment. The attack has a much better chance of success when the man's whole inner world is drab and cold and empty. And it is also to be noted that the Trough sexuality is subtly different in quality from that of the Peak—much less likely to lead to the milk-and-water phenomenon which the humans call "being in love," much more easily drawn into perversions, much less contaminated by those generous and imaginative and even spiritual concomitants which often render human sexuality so disappointing. It is the same with other desires of the flesh. You are much more likely to make your man a sound drunkard by pressing drink on him as an anodyne when he is dull and weary than by encouraging him to use it as a means of merriment among his friends when he is happy and expansive. Never forget that when we are dealing with any pleasure in its healthy and normal and satisfying form, we are, in a sense, on the Enemy's ground. I know we have won many a soul through pleasure. All the same, it is His invention, not ours. He made the pleasures: all our research so far has not enabled us to produce one. All we can do is to encourage the humans to take the pleasures which our Enemy has produced, at times, or in ways, or in degrees, which He has forbidden. Hence we always try to work away from the natural condition of any pleasure to that in which it is least natural, least redolent of its Maker, and least pleasurable. An ever increasing craving for an ever diminishing pleasure is the formula. It is more certain; and it's better *style.* To get the man's soul and give him *nothing* in return—that is what really gladdens our Father's heart. And the troughs are the time for beginning the process.

But there is an even better way of exploiting the Trough; I mean through the patient's own thoughts about it. As always, the first step is to keep knowledge out of his mind. Do not let him suspect the law of undulation. Let him assume that the first ardours of his conversion might have been expected to last, and ought to have lasted, forever, and that his present dryness is an equally permanent condition. Having once got this misconception well fixed in his head, you may then proceed in various ways. It all depends on whether your man is of the desponding type who can be tempted to despair, or of the wishful-thinking type who can be assured that all is well. The former type is getting rare among the humans. If your patient should happen to belong to it, everything is easy. You have only got to keep him out of the way of experienced Christians (an easy task nowadays), to direct his attention to the appropriate passages in Scripture, and then to set him to work on the desperate design of recovering his old feelings by sheer will power, and the game is ours. If he is of the more hopeful type, your job is to make him acquiesce in the present low temperature of his spirit and gradually become content with it, persuading himself that it is not so low after all. In a week or two you will be making him doubt whether the first days of his Christianity were not, perhaps, a little excessive. Talk to him about "moderation in all things." If you can once get him to the point of thinking that "religion is all very well up to a point," you can feel quite happy about his soul. A moderated religion is as good for us as no religion at all—and more amusing.

Another possibility is that of direct attack on his faith. When you have caused him to assume that the trough is permanent, can you not persuade him that "his religious phase" is just going to die away like all his previous phases? Of course there is no conceivable way of getting by reason from the proposition "I am losing interest in this" to the proposition "This is false." But, as I said before, it is jargon, not reason, you must rely on. The mere word *phase* will very likely do the trick. I assume that the creature has been through several of them before—they all have—and that he always feels superior and patronising to the ones he has emerged from, not because he has really criticised them but simply because they are in the past. (You keep him well fed on hazy ideas of Progress and Development and the Historical Point of View, I trust, and give him lots of modern biographies to read? The people in them are always emerging from Phases, aren't they?)

You see the idea? Keep his mind off the plain antithesis between True and False. Nice shadowy expressions—"It was a phase"—"I've been through all that"—and don't forget the blessed word "Adolescent."

Your affectionate uncle

SCREWTAPE

X

Influence of Friends

My dear Wormwood,

I was delighted to hear from Triptweeze that your patient has made some very desirable new acquaintances and that you seem to have used this event in a really promising manner. I gather that the middle-aged married couple who called at his office are just the sort of people we want him to know—rich, smart, superficially intellectual, and brightly sceptical about everything in the world. I gather they are even vaguely pacifist, not on moral grounds but from an ingrained habit of belittling anything that concerns the great mass of their fellow men and from a dash of purely fashionable and literary communism. This is excellent. And you seem to have made good use of all his social, sexual, and intellectual vanity. Tell me more. Did he commit himself deeply? I don't mean in words. There is a subtle play of looks and tones and laughs by which a mortal can imply that he is of the same party as those to whom he is speaking. That is the kind of betrayal you should specially encourage, because the man does not fully realise it himself; and by the time he does you will have made withdrawal difficult.

No doubt he must very soon realise that his own faith is in direct opposition to the assumptions on which all the conversation of his new friends is based. I don't think that matters much provided that you can persuade him to postpone any open acknowledgment of the fact, and this, with the aid of shame, pride, modesty and vanity, will be easy to do. As long as the postponement lasts he will be in a false position. He will be silent when he ought to speak and laugh when he ought to be silent. He will assume, at first only by his manner, but presently by his words, all sorts of cynical and sceptical attitudes which are not really his. But if you play him well, they may become his. All mortals tend to turn into the thing they are pretending to be. This is elementary. The real question is how to prepare for the Enemy's counterattack.

The first thing is to delay as long as possible the moment at which he realises this new pleasure as a temptation. Since the Enemy's servants have been preaching about "the World" as one of the great standard temptations for two thousand years, this might seem difficult to do. But fortunately they have said very little about it for the last few decades. In modern Christian writings, though I see much (indeed more than I like) about Mammon, I see few of the old warnings about Worldly Vanities, the Choice of Friends, and the Value of Time. All that, your patient would probably classify as "Puritanism"—and may I remark in

hypocrisy +shallowness of society

passing that the value we have given to that word is one of the really solid triumphs of the last hundred years? By it we rescue annually thousands of humans from temperance, chastity, and sobriety of life.

Sooner or later, however, the real nature of his new friends must become clear to him, and then your tactics must depend on the patient's intelligence. If he is a big enough fool you can get him to realise the character of the friends only while they are absent; their presence can be made to sweep away all criticism. If this succeeds, he can be induced to live, as I have known many humans live, for quite long periods, two parallel lives; he will not only appear to be, but actually be, a different man in each of the circles he frequents. Failing this, there is a subtler and more entertaining method. He can be made to take a positive pleasure in the perception that the two sides of his life are inconsistent. This is done by exploiting his vanity. He can be taught to enjoy kneeling beside the grocer on Sunday just because he remembers that the grocer could not possibly understand the urbane and mocking world which he inhabited on Saturday evening; and contrariwise, to enjoy the bawdy and blasphemy over the coffee with these admirable friends all the more because he is aware of a "deeper," "spiritual" world within him which they cannot understand. You see the idea—the worldly friends touch him on one side and the grocer on the other, and he is the complete, balanced, complex man who sees round them all. Thus, while being permanently treacherous to at least two sets of people, he will feel, instead of shame, a continual undercurrent of self-satisfaction. Finally, if all else fails, you can persuade him, in defiance of conscience, to continue the new acquaintance on the ground that he is, in some unspecified way, doing these people "good" by the mere fact of drinking their cocktails and laughing at their jokes, and that to cease to do so would be "priggish," "intolerant," and (of course) "Puritanical."

Meanwhile you will of course take the obvious precaution of seeing that this new development induces him to spend more than he can afford and to neglect his work and his mother. Her jealousy and alarm, and his increasing evasiveness or rudeness, will be invaluable for the aggravation of the domestic tension.

Your affectionate uncle

SCREWTAPE

XI

4 causes of Laughter.
Joy, Fun
Joke Proper, Flippancy

*M*y dear Wormwood,

Everything is clearly going very well. I am specially glad to hear that the two new friends have now made him acquainted with their whole set. All these, as I find from the record office, are thoroughly reliable people; steady, consistent scoffers and worldlings who without any spectacular crimes are progressing quietly and comfortably towards Our Father's house. You speak of their being great laughers. I trust this does not mean that you are under the impression that laughter as such is always in our favour. The point is worth some attention.

I divide the causes of human laughter into Joy, Fun, the Joke Proper, and Flippancy. You will see the first among friends and lovers reunited on the eve of a holiday. Among adults some pretext in the way of Jokes is usually provided, but the facility with which the smallest witticisms produce laughter at such a time shows that they are not the real cause. What that real cause is we do not know. Something like it is expressed in much of that detestable art which the humans call Music, and something like it occurs in Heaven—a meaningless acceleration in the rhythm of celestial experience, quite opaque to us. Laughter of this kind does us no good and should always be discouraged. Besides, the phenomenon is of itself disgusting and a direct insult to the realism, dignity, and austerity of Hell.

Fun is closely related to Joy—a sort of emotional froth arising from the play instinct. It is very little use to us. It can sometimes be used, of course, to divert humans from something else which the Enemy would like them to be feeling or doing: but in itself it has wholly undesirable tendencies; it promotes charity, courage, contentment, and many other evils.

The Joke Proper, which turns on sudden perception of incongruity, is a much more promising field. I am not thinking primarily of indecent or bawdy humour, which, though much relied upon by second-rate tempters, is often disappointing in its results. The truth is that humans are pretty clearly divided on this matter into two classes. There are some to whom "no passion is as serious as lust" and for whom an indecent story ceases to produce lasciviousness precisely in so far as it becomes funny: there are others in whom laughter and lust are excited at the same moment and by the same things. The first sort joke about sex because it gives rise to many incongruities; the second cultivate incongruities because they afford a pretext for talking about sex. If your man is of the first type, bawdy humour will not help you—I shall never forget the hours which I wasted (hours to me of unbearable tedium) with one of my early patients in bars and smoking rooms before I learned this rule. Find out which group the patient belongs to—and see that he does *not* find out.

The real use of Jokes or Humour is in quite a different direction, and it is specially promising among the English, who take their "sense of humour" so seriously that a deficiency in this sense is almost the only deficiency at which they feel shame. Humour is for them the all-consoling and (mark this) the all-excusing, grace of life. Hence it is invaluable as a means of destroying shame. If a man simply lets others pay for him, he is "mean"; if he boasts of it in a jocular manner and twits his fellows with having been scored off, he is no longer "mean" but a comical fellow. Mere cowardice is shameful; cowardice boasted of with humorous exaggerations and grotesque gestures can be passed off as funny. Cruelty is shameful—unless the cruel man can represent it as a practical joke. A thousand bawdy, or even blasphemous, jokes do not help towards a man's damnation so much as his discovery that almost anything he wants to do can be done, not only without the disapproval but with the admiration of his fellows, if only it can get itself treated as a Joke. And this temptation can be almost entirely hidden from your patient by that English seriousness about Humour. Any suggestion that there might be too much of it can be represented to him as "Puritanical" or as betraying a "lack of humour."

But flippancy is the best of all. In the first place

it is very economical. Only a clever human can make a real Joke about virtue, or indeed about anything else; any of them can be trained to talk *as if* virtue were funny. Among flippant people the Joke is always assumed to have been made. No one actually makes it; but every serious subject is discussed in a manner which implies that they have already found a ridiculous side to it. If prolonged, the habit of Flippancy builds up around a man the finest armour plating against the Enemy that I know, and it is quite free from the dangers inherent in the other sources of laughter. It is a thousand miles away from joy; it deadens, instead of sharpening, the intellect; and it excites no affection between those who practice it.

Your affectionate uncle

S<small>CREWTAPE</small>

XII

Unease

My dear Wormwood,

Obviously you are making excellent progress. My only fear is lest in attempting to hurry the patient you awaken him to a sense of his real position. For you and I, who see that position as it really is, must never forget how totally different it ought to appear to him. We know that we have introduced a change of direction in his course which is already carrying him out of his orbit around the Enemy; but he must be made to imagine that all the choices which have effected this change of course are trivial and revocable. He must not be allowed to suspect that he is now, however slowly, heading right away from the sun on a line which will carry him into the cold and dark of utmost space.

For this reason I am almost glad to hear that he is still a churchgoer and a communicant. I know there are dangers in this; but anything is better than that he should realise the break he has made with the first months of his Christian life. As long as he retains externally the habits of a Christian he can still be made to think of himself as one who has adopted a few new friends and amusements but whose spiritual state is much the same as it was six weeks ago. And while he thinks that, we do not have to contend with the explicit repentance of a definite, fully recognised, sin, but only with his vague, though uneasy, feeling that he hasn't been doing very well lately.

This dim uneasiness needs careful handling. If it gets too strong it may wake him up and spoil the whole game. On the other hand, if you suppress it entirely—which, by the by, the Enemy will probably not allow you to do—we lose an element in the situation which can be turned to good account. If such a feeling is allowed to live, but not allowed to become irresistible and flower into real repentance, it has one invaluable tendency. It increases the patient's reluctance to think about the Enemy. All humans at nearly all times have some such reluctance; but when thinking of Him involves facing and intensifying a whole vague cloud of half-conscious guilt, this reluctance is increased tenfold. They hate every idea that suggests Him, just as men in financial embarrassment hate the very sight of a bankbook. In this state your patient will not omit, but he will increasingly dislike, his religious duties. He will think about them as little as he feels he decently can beforehand, and forget them as soon as possible when they are over. A few weeks ago you had to *tempt* him to unreality and inattention in his prayers: but now you will find him opening his arms to you and almost begging you to distract his purpose and benumb his heart. He will *want* his prayers to be unreal, for he will dread nothing so much as effective contact with the Enemy. His aim will be to let sleeping worms lie.

As this condition becomes more fully established, you will be gradually freed from the tiresome business of providing Pleasures as temptations. As the uneasiness and his reluctance to face it cut him off more and more from all real happiness, and as habit renders the pleasures of vanity and excitement and flippancy at once less pleasant and harder to forgo (for that is what habit fortunately does to a pleasure) you will find that anything or nothing is sufficient to attract his wandering attention. You no longer need a good book, which he really likes, to keep him from his prayers or his work or his sleep; a column of advertisements in yesterday's paper will do. You can make him waste his time not only in conversation he enjoys with people whom he likes, but in conversations with those he cares nothing about, on subjects that bore him. You can make him do nothing at all for long periods. You can keep him up late at night, not roistering, but staring at a dead fire in a cold room. All the healthy and outgoing activities which we want him to avoid can be inhibited and *nothing* given in return, so that at last he may say, as one of my own patients said on his arrival down here, "I now see that I spent most of my life in doing *neither* what I ought *nor* what I liked." The Christians describe the Enemy as one "without whom Nothing is strong." And Nothing is very strong: strong enough to steal away a man's best years not in sweet sins but in a dreary flickering of the mind over it knows not what and knows not why, in the gratification of curiosities so feeble that the man is only half aware of them, in drumming of fingers and kicking of heels, in whistling tunes that he does not like, or in the long, dim labyrinth of reveries that have not even lust or ambition to give them a relish, but which, once chance association has started them, the creature is too weak and fuddled to shake off.

You will say that these are very small sins; and doubtless, like all young tempters, you are anxious to be able to report spectacular wickedness. But do remember, the only thing that matters is the extent to which you separate the man from the Enemy. It does not matter how small the sins are, provided that their cumulative effect is to edge the man away from the Light and out into the Nothing. Murder is no better than cards if cards can do the trick. Indeed the safest road to Hell is the gradual one—the gentle slope, soft underfoot, without sudden turnings, without milestones, without signposts.

Your affectionate uncle

SCREWTAPE

XIII

*M*y dear Wormwood,

It seems to me that you take a great many pages to tell a very simple story. The long and the short of it is that you have let the man slip through your fingers. The situation is very grave, and I really see no reason why I should try to shield you from the consequences of your inefficiency. A repentance and renewal of what the other side call "grace" on the scale which you describe is a defeat of the first order. It amounts to a second conversion—and probably on a deeper level than the first.

As you ought to have known, the asphyxiating cloud which prevented your attacking the patient on his walk back from the old mill is a well-known phenomenon. It is the Enemy's most barbarous weapon, and generally appears when He is directly present to the patient under certain modes not yet fully classified. Some humans are permanently surrounded by it and therefore inaccessible to us.

And now for your blunders. On your own showing you first of all allowed the patient to read a book he really enjoyed, because he enjoyed it and not in order to make clever remarks about it to his new friends. In the second place, you allowed him to walk down to the old mill and have tea there—a walk through country he really likes, and taken alone. In other words you allowed him two real positive Pleasures. Were you so ignorant as not to see the danger of this? The characteristic of Pains and Pleasures is that they are unmistakably real, and therefore, as far as they go, give the man who feels them a touchstone of reality. Thus if you had been trying to damn your man by the Romantic method—by making him a kind of Childe Harold or Werther submerged in self-pity for imaginary distresses—you would try to protect him at all costs from any real pain; because, of course, five minutes' genuine toothache would reveal the romantic sorrows for the nonsense they were and unmask your whole stratagem. But you were trying to damn your patient by the World, that is, by palming off vanity, bustle, irony, and expensive tedium as pleasures. How can you have failed to see that a *real* pleasure was the last thing you ought to have let him meet? Didn't you foresee that it would just kill by contrast all the trumpery which you have been so laboriously teaching him to value? And that the sort of pleasure which the book and the walk gave him was the most dangerous of all? That it would peel off from his sensibility the kind of crust you have been forming on it, and make him feel that he was coming home, recovering himself? As a preliminary to detaching him from the Enemy, you wanted to detach him from himself, and had made some progress in doing so. Now, all that is undone.

Of course I know that the Enemy also wants to detach men from themselves, but in a different way. Remember always, that He really likes the little vermin, and sets an absurd value on the distinctness of every one of them. When He talks of their losing their selves, He only means abandoning the clamour of self-will; once they have done that, He really gives them back all their personality, and boasts (I am afraid, sincerely) that when they are wholly His they will be more themselves than ever. Hence, while He is delighted to see them sacrificing even their innocent wills to His, He hates to see them drifting away from their own nature for any other reason. And we should always encourage them to do so. The deepest likings and impulses of any man are the raw material, the starting point, with which the Enemy has furnished him. To get him away from those is therefore always a point gained; even in things indifferent it is always desirable to substitute the standards of the World, or convention, or fashion, for a human's own real likings and dislikings. I myself would carry this very far. I would make it a rule to eradicate from my patient any strong personal taste which is not actually a sin, even if it is something quite trivial such as a fondness for county cricket or collecting stamps or drinking cocoa. Such things, I grant you, have nothing of virtue in them; but there is a sort of innocence and humility and self-forgetfulness about them which I distrust. The man who truly and disinter-

Personalities → don't be yourself.

estedly enjoys any one thing in the world, for its own sake, and without caring twopence what other people say about it, is by that very fact forearmed against some of our subtlest modes of attack. You should always try to make the patient abandon the people or food or books he really likes in favour of the "best" people, the "right" food, the "important" books. I have known a human defended from strong temptations to social ambition by a still stronger taste for tripe and onions.

It remains to consider how we can retrieve this disaster. The great thing is to prevent his doing anything. As long as he does not convert it into action, it does not matter how much he thinks about this new repentance. Let the little brute wallow in it. Let him, if he has any bent that way, write a book about it; that is often an excellent way of sterilising the seeds which the Enemy plants in a human soul. Let him do anything but act. No amount of piety in his imagination and affections will harm us if we can keep it out of his will. As one of the humans has said, active habits are strengthened by repetition but passive ones are weakened. The more often he feels without acting, the less he will be able ever to act, and, in the long run, the less he will be able to feel.

Your affectionate uncle

SCREWTAPE

XIV

humility –

My dear Wormwood,

The most alarming thing in your last account of the patient is that he is making none of those confident resolutions which marked his original conversion. No more lavish promises of perpetual virtue, I gather; not even the expectation of an endowment of "grace" for life, but only a hope for the daily and hourly pittance to meet the daily and hourly temptation! This is very bad.

I see only one thing to do at the moment. Your patient has become humble; have you drawn his attention to the fact? All virtues are less formidable to us once the man is aware that he has them, but this is specially true of humility. Catch him at the moment when he is really poor in spirit and smuggle into his mind the gratifying reflection, "By jove! I'm being humble," and almost immediately pride—pride at his own humility—will appear. If he awakes to the danger and tries to smother this new form of pride, make him proud of his attempt—and so on, through as many stages as you please. But don't try this too long, for fear you awake his sense of humour and proportion, in which case he will merely laugh at you and go to bed.

But there are other profitable ways of fixing his attention on the virtue of Humility. By this virtue, as by all the others, our Enemy wants to turn the man's attention away from self to Him, and to the man's neighbours. All the abjection and self-hatred are designed, in the long run, solely for this end; unless they attain this end they do us little harm; and they may even do us good if they keep the man concerned with himself, and, above all, if self-contempt can be made the starting point for contempt of other selves, and thus for gloom, cynicism, and cruelty.

You must therefore conceal from the patient the true end of Humility. Let him think of it, not as self-forgetfulness but as a certain kind of opinion (namely, a low opinion) of his own talents and character. Some talents, I gather, he really has. Fix in his mind the idea that humility consists in trying to believe those talents to be less valuable than he believes them to be. No doubt they *are* in fact less valuable than he believes, but that is not the point. The great thing is to make him value an opinion for some quality other than truth, thus introducing an element of dishonesty and make-believe into the heart of what otherwise threatens to become a virtue. By this method thousands of humans have been brought to think that humility means pretty women trying to believe they are ugly and clever men trying to believe they are fools. And since what they are trying to believe may, in some cases, be manifest nonsense, they cannot succeed in believing it and we have the chance of keeping their minds endlessly revolving on themselves in an effort to achieve the impossible. To anticipate the Enemy's strategy, we must consider His aims. The Enemy wants to bring the man to a state of mind in which he could design the best cathedral in the world, and know it to be the best, and rejoice in the fact, without being any more (or less) or otherwise glad at having done it than he would be if it had been done by another. The Enemy wants him, in the end, to be so free from any bias in his own favour that he can rejoice in his own talents as frankly and gratefully as in his neighbour's talents—or in a sunrise, an elephant, or a waterfall. He wants each man, in the long run, to be able to recognise all creatures (even himself) as glorious and excellent things. He wants to kill their animal self-love as soon as possible; but it is His long-term policy, I fear, to restore to them a new kind of self-love—a charity and gratitude for all selves, including their own; when they have really learned to love their neighbours as themselves, they will be allowed to love themselves as their neighbours. For we must never forget what is the most repellent and inexplicable trait in our Enemy; He *really* loves the hairless bipeds He has created, and always gives back to them with His right hand what He has taken away with His left.

His whole effort, therefore, will be to get the man's mind off the subject of his own value altogether. He would rather the man thought himself a great architect or a great poet and then forgot about it, than that he should spend much time and pains trying to think himself a bad one. Your efforts to instil either vainglory or false modesty into the patient will therefore be met from the Enemy's side with the obvious reminder that a man is not usually called upon to have an opinion of his own talents at all, since he can very well go on improving them to the best of his ability without deciding on his own precise niche in the temple of Fame. You must try to exclude this reminder from the patient's consciousness at all costs. The Enemy will also try to render real in the patient's mind a doctrine which they all profess but find it difficult to bring home to their feelings—the doctrine that they did not create themselves, that their talents were given them, and that they might as well be proud of the colour of their hair. But always and by all methods the Enemy's aim will be to get the patient's mind off such questions, and yours will be to fix it on them. Even of his sins the Enemy does not want him to think too much: once they are repented, the sooner the man turns his attention outward, the better the Enemy is pleased.

Your affectionate uncle

SCREWTAPE

XV

*M*y dear Wormwood,

I had noticed, of course, that the humans were having a lull in their European war—what they naïvely call *"The War!"*—and am not surprised that there is a corresponding lull in the patient's anxieties. Do we want to encourage this, or to keep him worried? Tortured fear and stupid confidence are both desirable states of mind. Our choice between them raises important questions.

The humans live in time but our Enemy destines them to eternity. He therefore, I believe, wants them to attend chiefly to two things, to eternity itself, and to that point of time which they call the Present. For the Present is the point at which time touches eternity. Of the present moment, and of it only, humans have an experience analogous to the experience which our Enemy has of reality as a whole; in it alone freedom and actuality are offered them. He would therefore have them continually concerned either with eternity (which means being concerned with Him) or with the Present—either meditating on their eternal union with, or separation from, Himself, or else obeying the present voice of conscience, bearing the present cross, receiving the present grace, giving thanks for the present pleasure.

Our business is to get them away from the eternal, and from the Present. With this in view, we sometimes tempt a human (say a widow or a scholar) to live in the Past. But this is of limited value, for they have some real knowledge of the Past and it has a determinate nature and, to that extent, resembles eternity. It is far better to make them live in the Future. Biological necessity makes all their passions point in that direction already, so that thought about the Future inflames hope and fear. Also, it is unknown to them, so that in making them think about it we make them think of unrealities. In a word, the Future is, of all things, the thing *least like* eternity. It is the most completely temporal part of time—for the Past is frozen and no longer flows, and the Present is all lit up with eternal rays. Hence the encouragement we have given to all those schemes of thought such as Creative Evolution, Scientific Humanism, or Communism, which fix men's affections on the Future, on the very core of temporality. Hence nearly all vices are rooted in the Future. Gratitude looks to the Past and love to the Present; fear, avarice, lust, and ambition look ahead. Do not think lust an exception. When the present pleasure arrives, the sin (which alone interests us) is already over. The pleasure is just the part of the process which we regret and would exclude if we could do so without losing the sin; it is the part contributed by the Enemy, and therefore experienced in a Present. The sin, which is our contribution, looked forward.

To be sure, the Enemy wants men to think of the Future too—just so much as is necessary for *now* planning the acts of justice or charity which will probably be their duty tomorrow. The duty of planning the morrow's work is *today's* duty; though its material is borrowed from the future, the duty, like all duties, is in the Present. This is not straw splitting. He does not want men to give the Future their hearts, to place their treasure in it. We do. His ideal is a man who, having worked all day for the good of posterity (if that is his vocation), washes his mind of the whole subject, commits the issue to Heaven, and returns at once to the patience or gratitude demanded by the moment that is passing over him. But we want a man hagridden by the Future—haunted by visions of an imminent heaven or hell upon earth—ready to break the Enemy's commands in the Present if by so doing we make him think he can attain the one or avert the other—dependent for his faith on the success or failure of schemes whose end he will not live to see. We want a whole race perpetually in pursuit of the rainbow's end, never honest, nor kind, nor happy *now*, but always using as mere fuel wherewith to heap the altar of the Future every real gift which is offered them in the Present.

It follows, then, in general, and other things being equal, that it is better for your patient to be filled with anxiety or hope (it doesn't much matter which) about this war than for him to be living in the Present. But the phrase "living in the Present" is ambiguous. It may describe a process which is really just as much concerned with the Future as anxiety itself. Your man may be untroubled about the Future, not because he is concerned with the Present, but because he has persuaded himself that the Future is going to be agreeable. As long as that is the real course of his tranquillity, his tranquillity will do us good, because it is only piling up more disappointment, and therefore more impatience, for him when his false hopes are dashed. If, on the other hand, he is aware that horrors may be in store for him and is praying for the virtues wherewith to meet them, and meanwhile concerning himself with the Present because there, and there alone, all duty, all grace, all knowledge, and all pleasure dwell, his state is very undesirable and should be attacked at once. Here again, our Philological Arm has done good work; try the word "complacency" on him. But, of course, it is most likely that he is "living in the Present" for none of these reasons but simply because his health is good and he is enjoying his work. The phenomenon would then be merely natural. All the same, I should break it up if I were you. No natural phenomenon is really in our favour. And anyway, why *should* the creature be happy?

Your affectionate uncle
SCREWTAPE

XVI

Church

*M*y dear Wormwood,

You mentioned casually in your last letter that the patient has continued to attend one church, and one only, since he was converted, and that he is not wholly pleased with it. May I ask what you are about? Why have I no report on the causes of his fidelity to the parish church? Do you realise that unless it is due to indifference it is a very bad thing? Surely you know that if a man can't be cured of churchgoing, the next best thing is to send him all over the neighbourhood looking for the church that "suits" him until he becomes a taster or connoisseur of churches.

The reasons are obvious. In the first place the parochial organisation should always be attacked, because, being a unity of place and not of likings, it brings people of different classes and psychology together in the kind of unity the Enemy desires. The congregational principle, on the other hand, makes each church into a kind of club, and finally, if all goes well, into a coterie or faction. In the second place, the search for a "suitable" church makes the man a critic where the Enemy wants

him to be a pupil. What He wants of the layman
in church is an attitude which may, indeed, be
critical in the sense of rejecting what is false or
unhelpful, but which is wholly uncritical in the
sense that it does not appraise—does not waste
time in thinking about what it rejects, but lays
itself open in uncommenting, humble receptivity
to any nourishment that is going. (You see how
grovelling, how unspiritual, how irredeemably vulgar He is!) This attitude, especially during ser-
mons, creates the condition (most hostile to our
whole policy) in which platitudes can become really audible to a human soul. There is hardly any
sermon, or any book, which may not be dangerous to us if it is received in this temper. So pray
bestir yourself and send this fool the round of the
neighbouring churches as soon as possible. Your
record up to date has not given us much satis-
faction.

The two churches nearest to him, I have looked
up in the office. Both have certain claims. At the
first of these the vicar is a man who has been so
long engaged in watering down the faith to make
it easier for a supposedly incredulous and hard-
headed congregation that it is now he who shocks
his parishioners with his unbelief, not *vice versa*.
He has undermined many a soul's Christianity.
His conduct of the services is also admirable. In
order to spare the laity all "difficulties" he has
deserted both the lectionary and the appointed
psalms and now, without noticing it, revolves endlessly round the little treadmill of his fifteen favourite psalms and twenty favourite lessons. We

are thus safe from the danger that any truth not already familiar to him and to his flock should ever reach them through Scripture. But perhaps your patient is not quite silly enough for this church—or not yet?

At the other church we have Fr. Spike. The humans are often puzzled to understand the range of his opinions—why he is one day almost a Communist and the next not far from some kind of theocratic Fascism—one day a scholastic, and the next prepared to deny human reason altogether—one day immersed in politics, and, the day after, declaring that all states of this world are *equally* "under judgment." We, of course, see the connecting link, which is Hatred. The man cannot bring himself to preach anything which is not calculated to shock, grieve, puzzle, or humiliate his parents and their friends. A sermon which such people could accept would be to him as insipid as a poem which they could scan. There is also a promising streak of dishonesty in him; we are teaching him to say "The teaching of the Church is" when he really means "I'm almost sure I read recently in Maritain or someone of that sort." But I must warn you that he has one fatal defect: he really believes. And this may yet mar all.

But there is one good point which both these churches have in common—they are both party churches. I think I warned you before that if your patient can't be kept out of the Church, he ought at least to be violently attached to some party within it. I don't mean on really doctrinal issues; about those, the more lukewarm he is the better.

And it isn't the doctrines on which we chiefly depend for producing malice. The real fun is working up hatred between those who *say* "mass" and those who *say* "holy communion" when neither party could possibly state the difference between, say, Hooker's doctrine and Thomas Aquinas', in any form which would hold water for five minutes. And all the purely indifferent things—candles and clothes and what not—are an admirable ground for our activities. We have quite removed from men's minds what that pestilent fellow Paul used to teach about food and other unessentials— namely, that the human without scruples should always give in to the human with scruples. You would think they could not fail to see the application. You would expect to find the "low" churchman genuflecting and crossing himself lest the weak conscience of his "high" brother should be moved to irreverence, and the "high" one refraining from these exercises lest he should betray his "low" brother into idolatry. And so it would have been but for our ceaseless labour. Without that, the variety of usage within the Church of England might have become a positive hotbed of charity and humility.

Your affectionate uncle
Screwtape

XVII

*M*y dear Wormwood,

The contemptuous way in which you spoke of gluttony as a means of catching souls, in your last letter, shows only your ignorance. One of the great achievements of the last hundred years has been to deaden the human conscience on that subject, so that by now you will hardly find a sermon preached or a conscience troubled about it in the whole length and breadth of Europe. This has largely been effected by concentrating all our efforts on gluttony of Delicacy, not gluttony of Excess. Your patient's mother, as I learn from the dossier and you might have learned from Glubose, is a good example. She would be astonished—one day, I hope, *will* be—to learn that her whole life is enslaved to this kind of sensuality, which is quite concealed from her by the fact that the quantities involved are small. But what do quantities matter, provided we can use a human belly and palate to produce querulousness, impatience, uncharitableness, and self-concern? Glubose has this old woman well in hand. She is a positive terror to hostesses and servants. She is always turning from what has been offered her to say with a demure little sigh and a smile, "Oh please, please . . . *all* I want is a cup of tea, weak but not too weak, and the teeniest weeniest bit of really crisp toast." You see? Because what she wants is smaller and less costly than what has been set before her, she never recognises as gluttony her determination to get what she wants, however troublesome it may be to others. At the very moment of indulging her appetite she believes that she is practising temperance. In a crowded restaurant she gives a little scream at the plate which some overworked waitress has set before her and says: "Oh, that's far, far too much! Take it away and bring me about a quarter of it." If challenged, she would say she was doing this to avoid waste; in reality she does it because the particular shade of delicacy to which we have enslaved her is offended by the sight of more food than she happens to want.

The real value of the quiet, unobtrusive work which Glubose has been doing for years on this old woman can be gauged by the way in which her belly now dominates her whole life. The woman is in what may be called the "All-I-want" state of mind. *All* she wants is a cup of tea properly made, or an egg properly boiled, or a slice of bread properly toasted. But she never finds any servant or any friend who can do these simple things "properly"—because her "properly" conceals an insatiable demand for the exact, and almost impossible, palatal pleasures which she imagines she remembers from the past; a past described by her as "the days when you could get good servants" but known to us as the days when her senses were more easily pleased and she had pleasures of other kinds which made her less dependent on those of the table. Meanwhile, the daily disappointment produces daily ill temper: cooks give notice and friendships are cooled. If ever the Enemy introduces into her mind a faint suspicion that she is too interested in food, Glubose counters it by suggesting to her that she doesn't mind what she eats herself but "does like to have things nice for her boy." In fact, of course, her greed has been one of the chief sources of his domestic discomfort for many years.

Now, your patient is his mother's son. While working your hardest, quite rightly, on other fronts, you must not neglect a little quiet infiltration in respect of gluttony. Being a male, he is not so likely to be caught by the "*All*-I-want" camouflage. Males are best turned into gluttons with the help of their vanity. They ought to be made to think themselves very knowing about food, to pique themselves on having found the only restaurant in the town where steaks are really "properly" cooked. What begins as vanity can then be gradually turned into habit. But, however you approach it, the great thing is to bring him into the state in which the denial of any one indulgence—it matters not which, champagne or tea, *sole Colbert* or cigarettes—"puts him out," for then his charity, justice, and obedience are all at your mercy.

Mere excess in food is much less valuable than delicacy. Its chief use is as a kind of artillery preparation for attacks on chastity. On that, as on every other subject, keep your man in a condition of false spirituality. Never let him notice the medical aspect. Keep him wondering what pride or lack of faith has delivered him into your hands when a simple enquiry into what he has been eating or drinking for the last twenty-four hours would show him whence your ammunition comes and thus enable him by a very little abstinence to imperil your lines of communication. If he *must* think of the medical side of chastity, feed him the grand lie which we have made the English humans believe, that physical exercise in excess and consequent fatigue are specially favourable to this virtue. How they can believe this, in face of the notorious lustfulness of sailors and soldiers, may well be asked. But we used the schoolmasters to put the story about—men who were really interested in chastity as an excuse for games and therefore recommended games as an aid to chastity. But this whole business is too large to deal with at the tail end of a letter.

Your affectionate uncle

SCREWTAPE

XVIII

*M*y dear Wormwood,

Even under Slubgob you must have learned at college the routine technique of sexual temptation, and since, for us spirits, this whole subject is one of considerable tedium (though necessary as part of our training) I will pass it over. But on the larger issues involved I think you have a good deal to learn.

The Enemy's demand on humans takes the form of a dilemma; *either* complete abstinence or unmitigated monogamy. Ever since Our Father's first great victory, we have rendered the former very difficult to them. The latter, for the last few centuries, we have been closing up as a way of escape. We have done this through the poets and novelists by persuading the humans that a curious, and usually short-lived, experience which they call "being in love" is the only respectable ground for marriage; that marriage can, and ought to, render this excitement permanent; and that a marriage which does not do so is no longer binding. This idea is our parody of an idea that came from the Enemy.

The whole philosophy of Hell rests on recognition of the axiom that one thing is not another thing, and, specially, that one self is not another self. My good is my good and your good is yours. What one gains another loses. Even an inanimate object is what it is by excluding all other objects from the space it occupies; if it expands, it does so by thrusting other objects aside or by absorbing them. A self does the same. With beasts the absorption takes the form of eating; for us, it means the sucking of will and freedom out of a weaker self into a stronger. "To be" *means* "to be in competition."

Now, the Enemy's philosophy is nothing more nor less than one continued attempt to evade this very obvious truth. He aims at a contradiction. Things are to be many, yet somehow also one. The good of one self is to be the good of another. This impossibility He calls *Love*, and this same monotonous panacea can be detected under all He does and even all He is—or claims to be. Thus He is not content, even Himself, to be a sheer arithmetical unity; He claims to be three as well as one, in order that this nonsense about Love may find a foothold in His own nature. At the other end of the scale, He introduces into matter that obscene invention the organism, in which the parts are perverted from their natural destiny of competition and made to cooperate.

His real motive for fixing on sex as the method of reproduction among humans is only too apparent from the use He has made of it. Sex might have been, from our point of view, quite innocent.

It might have been merely one more mode in which a stronger self preyed upon a weaker—as it is, indeed, among the spiders where the bride concludes her nuptials by eating her groom. But in the humans the Enemy has gratuitously associated affection between the parties with sexual desire. He has also made the offspring dependent on the parents and given the parents an impulse to support it—thus producing the Family, which is like the organism, only worse; for the members are more distinct, yet also united in a more conscious and responsible way. The whole thing, in fact, turns out to be simply one more device for dragging in Love.

Now comes the joke. The Enemy described a married couple as "one flesh." He did not say "a happily married couple" or "a couple who married because they were in love," but you can make the humans ignore that. You can also make them forget that the man they call Paul did not confine it to *married* couples. Mere copulation, for him, makes "one flesh." You can thus get the humans to accept as rhetorical eulogies of "being in love" what were in fact plain descriptions of the real significance of sexual intercourse. The truth is that wherever a man lies with a woman, there, whether they like it or not, a transcendental relation is set up between them which must be eternally enjoyed or eternally endured. From the true statement that this transcendental relation was intended to produce—and, if obediently entered into, too often *will* produce—affection and the family, humans can be made to infer the false belief that the blend of affection, fear, and desire which they call "being in love" is the only thing that makes marriage either happy or holy. The error is easy to produce because "being in love" does very often, in Western Europe, precede marriages which are made in obedience to the Enemy's designs, that is, with the intention of fidelity, fertility and good will; just as religious emotion very often, but not always, attends conversion. In other words, the humans are to be encouraged to regard as the basis for marriage a highly coloured and distorted version of something the Enemy really promises as its result. Two advantages follow. In the first place, humans who have not the gift of continence can be deterred from seeking marriage as a solution because they do not find themselves "in love," and, thanks to us, the idea of marrying with any other motive seems to them low and cynical. Yes, they think that. They regard the intention of loyalty to a partnership for mutual help, for the preservation of chastity, and for the transmission of life, as something lower than a storm of emotion. (Don't neglect to make your man think the marriage service very offensive.) In the second place any sexual infatuation whatever, so long as it intends marriage, will be regarded as "love," and "love" will be held to excuse a man from all the guilt, and to protect him from all the consequences, of marrying a heathen, a fool, or a wanton. But more of this in my next.

Your affectionate uncle

SCREWTAPE

XIX

love of God

My dear Wormwood,

I have been thinking very hard about the question in your last letter. If, as I have clearly shown, all selves are by their very nature in competition, and therefore the Enemy's idea of Love is a contradiction in terms, what becomes of my reiterated warning that He really loves the human vermin and really desires their freedom and continued existence? I hope, my dear boy, you have not shown my letters to anyone. Not that it matters of course. Anyone would see that the appearance of heresy into which I have fallen is purely accidental. By the way, I hope you understood, too, that some apparently uncomplimentary references to Slubgob were purely jocular. I really have the highest respect for him. And, of course, some things I said about not shielding you from the authorities were not seriously meant. You can trust me to look after your interests. But do keep everything under lock and key.

The truth is I slipped by mere carelessness into saying that the Enemy really loves the humans. That, of course, is an impossibility. He is one being; they are distinct from Him. Their good cannot be His. All His talk about Love must be a disguise for something else—He must have some *real* motive for creating them and taking so much trouble about them. The reason one comes to talk as if He really had this impossible Love is our utter failure to find out that real motive. What does He stand to make out of them? That is the insoluble question. I do not see that it can do any harm to tell you that this very problem was a chief cause of Our Father's quarrel with the Enemy. When the creation of man was first mooted and when, even at that stage, the Enemy freely confessed that he foresaw a certain episode about a cross, Our Father very naturally sought an interview and asked for an explanation. The Enemy gave no reply except to produce the cock-and-bull story about disinterested Love which He has been circulating ever since. This Our Father naturally could not accept. He implored the Enemy to lay His cards on the table, and gave Him every opportunity. He admitted that he felt a real anxiety to know the secret; the Enemy replied, "I wish with all my heart that you did." It was, I imagine, at this stage in the interview that Our Father's disgust at such an unprovoked lack of confidence caused him to remove himself an infinite distance from the Presence with a suddenness which has given rise to the ridiculous enemy story that he was forcibly thrown out of Heaven. Since then, we have begun to see why our Oppressor was so secretive. His throne depends on the secret. Members of His faction have frequently admitted that if ever we came to understand what He means by Love, the war would be over and we should re-enter Heaven. And there lies the great task. We know that He cannot really love: nobody can; it doesn't make sense. If we could only find out what He is *really* up to! Hypothesis after hypothesis has been tried, and still we can't find out. Yet we must never lose hope; more and more complicated theories, fuller and fuller collections of data, richer rewards for researchers who make progress, more and more terrible punishments for those who fail—all this, pursued and accelerated to the very end of time, cannot, surely, fail to succeed.

You complain that my last letter does not make it clear whether I regard *being in love* as a desirable state for a human or not. But really, Wormwood, that is the sort of question one expects *them* to ask! Leave them to discuss whether "Love," or patriotism, or celibacy, or candles on altars, or teetotalism, or education, are "good" or "bad." Can't you see there's no answer? Nothing matters at all except the tendency of a given state of mind, in given circumstances, to move a particular patient at a particular moment nearer to the Enemy or nearer to us. Thus it would be quite a good thing to make the patient decide that Love is "good" or "bad." If he is an arrogant man with a contempt for the body really based on delicacy but mistaken by him for purity—and one who takes pleasure in flouting what most of his fellows approve—by all means let him decide against Love. Instil into him an overweening asceticism and then, when you have separated his sexuality from all that might humanise it, weigh in on him with it in some much more brutal and cynical form. If, on the other hand, he is an emotional, gullible man, feed him on minor poets and fifth-rate novelists of the old school until you have made him believe that "Love" is both irresistible and somehow intrinsically meritorious. This belief is not much help, I grant you, in producing casual unchastity; but it is an incomparable recipe for prolonged "noble," romantic, tragic adulteries, ending, if all goes well, in murders and suicides. Failing that, it can be used to steer the patient into a useful marriage. For marriage, though the Enemy's invention, has its uses. There must be several young women in your patient's neighbourhood who would render the Christian life intensely difficult to him if only you could persuade him to marry one of them. Please send me a report on this when you next write. In the meantime, get it quite clear in your own mind that this state of *falling in love* is not, in itself, necessarily favourable either to us or to the other side. It is simply an occasion which we and the Enemy are both trying to exploit. Like most of the other things which humans are excited about, such as health and sickness, age and youth, or war and peace, it is, from the point of view of the spiritual life, mainly raw material.

Your affectionate uncle

SCREWTAPE

XX

*M*y dear Wormwood,

I note with great displeasure that the Enemy has, for the time being, put a forcible end to your direct attacks on the patient's chastity. You ought to have known that He always does in the end, and you ought to have stopped before you reached that stage. For as things are, your man has now discovered the dangerous truth that these attacks don't last forever; consequently you cannot use again what is, after all, our best weapon—the belief of ignorant humans that there is no hope of getting rid of us except by yielding. I suppose you've tried persuading him that chastity is unhealthy?

I haven't yet got a report from you on young women in the neighbourhood. I should like it at once, for if we can't use his sexuality to make him unchaste we must try to use it for the promotion of a desirable marriage. In the meantime I should like to give you some hint about the type of woman—I mean the physical type—which he should be encouraged to fall in love with if "falling in love" is the best we can manage.

In a rough-and-ready way, of course, this question is decided for us by spirits far deeper down in the Lowerarchy than you and I. It is the business of these great masters to produce in every age a general misdirection of what may be called sexual "taste." This they do by working through the small circle of popular artists, dressmakers, actresses, and advertisers who determine the fashionable type. The aim is to guide each sex away from those members of the other with whom spiritually helpful, happy, and fertile marriages are most likely. Thus we have now for many centuries triumphed over nature to the extent of making certain secondary characteristics of the male (such as the beard) disagreeable to nearly all the females— and there is more in that than you might suppose. As regards the male taste we have varied a good deal. At one time we have directed it to the statuesque and aristocratic type of beauty, mixing men's vanity with their desires and encouraging the race to breed chiefly from the most arrogant and prodigal women. At another, we have selected an exaggeratedly feminine type, faint and languishing, so that folly and cowardice, and all the general falseness and littleness of mind which go with them, shall be at a premium. At present we are on the opposite tack. The age of jazz has succeeded the age of the waltz, and we now teach men to like women whose bodies are scarcely distinguishable from those of boys. Since this is a kind of beauty even more transitory than most, we thus aggravate the female's chronic horror of growing old (with many excellent results) and render her less willing and less able to bear children. And that is not all. We have engineered a great increase in the licence which society allows to the representation of the apparent nude (not the real nude) in art, and its exhibition on the stage or the bathing beach. It is all a fake, of course; the figures in the popular art are falsely drawn; the real women in bathing suits or tights are actually pinched in and propped up to make them appear firmer and more slender and more boyish than nature allows a full-grown woman to be. Yet at the same time, the modern world is taught to believe that it is being "frank" and "healthy" and getting back to nature. As a result we are more and more directing the desires of men to something which does not exist—making the rôle of the eye in sexuality more and more important and at the same time making its demands more and more impossible. What follows you can easily forecast!

That is the general strategy of the moment. But inside that framework you will still find it possible to encourage your patient's desires in one of two directions. You will find, if you look carefully into any human's heart, that he is haunted by at least two imaginary women—a terrestrial and an infernal Venus, and that his desire differs qualitatively according to its object. There is one type for which his desire is such as to be naturally amenable to the Enemy—readily mixed with charity, readily obedient to marriage, coloured all through with that golden light of reverence and naturalness which we detest; there is another type which he desires brutally, and desires to desire brutally, a type best used to draw him away from marriage altogether but which, even within marriage, he would tend to treat as a slave, an idol, or an accomplice. His love for the first might involve what the Enemy calls evil, but only accidentally; the man would wish that she was not someone else's wife and be sorry that he could not love her lawfully. But in the second type, the felt evil is what he wants; it is that "tang" in the flavour which he is after. In the face, it is the visible animality, or sulkiness or craft or cruelty, which he likes, and in the body, something quite different from what he ordinarily calls Beauty, something he may even, in a sane hour, describe as ugliness, but which, by our art, can be made to play on the raw nerve of his private obsession.

The real use of the infernal Venus is, no doubt, as prostitute or mistress. But if your man is a Christian, and if he has been well trained in nonsense about irresistible and all-excusing "Love," he can often be induced to marry her. And that is very well worth bringing about. You will have failed as regards fornication and solitary vice; but there are other, and more indirect, methods of using a man's sexuality to his undoing. And, by the way, they are not only efficient, but delightful; the unhappiness produced is of a very lasting and exquisite kind.

                              Your affectionate uncle
                                          SCREWTAPE

XXI

Tempting him w/ woman

*M*y dear Wormwood,

Yes. A period of sexual temptation is an excellent time for working in a subordinate attack on the patient's peevishness. It may even be the main attack, as long as he thinks it the subordinate one. But here, as in everything else, the way must be prepared for your moral assault by darkening his intellect.

Men are not angered by mere misfortune but by misfortune conceived as injury. And the sense of injury depends on the feeling that a legitimate claim has been denied. The more claims on life, therefore, that your patient can be induced to make, the more often he will feel injured and, as a result, ill-tempered. Now you will have noticed that nothing throws him into a passion so easily as to find a tract of time which he reckoned on having at his own disposal unexpectedly taken from him. It is the unexpected visitor (when he looked forward to a quiet evening), or the friend's talkative wife (turning up when he looked forward to a *tête-à-tête* with the friend), that throw him out of gear. Now he is not yet so uncharitable or

Satan can use demands on time to get D angry

slothful that these small demands on his courtesy are *in themselves* too much for it. They anger him because he regards his time as his own and feels that it is being stolen. You must therefore zealously guard in his mind the curious assumption "My time is my own." Let him have the feeling that he starts each day as the lawful possessor of twenty-four hours. Let him feel as a grievous tax that portion of this property which he has to make over to his employers, and as a generous donation that further portion which he allows to religious duties. But what he must never be permitted to doubt is that the total from which these deductions have been made was, in some mysterious sense, his own personal birthright.

You have here a delicate task. The assumption which you want him to go on making is so absurd that, if once it is questioned, even we cannot find a shred of argument in its defence. The man can neither make, nor retain, one moment of time; it all comes to him by pure gift; he might as well regard the sun and moon as his chattels. He is also, in theory, committed to a total service of the Enemy; and if the Enemy appeared to him in bodily form and demanded that total service for even one day, he would not refuse. He would be greatly relieved if that one day involved nothing harder than listening to the conversation of a foolish woman; and he would be relieved almost to the pitch of disappointment if for one half-hour in that day the Enemy said, "Now you may go and amuse yourself." Now, if he thinks about his assumption for a moment, even he is bound to real-

OWERNESHIP - God OWNS IT ALL

ise that he is actually in this situation every day. When I speak of preserving this assumption in his mind, therefore, the last thing I mean you to do is to furnish him with arguments in its defence. There aren't any. Your task is purely negative. Don't let his thoughts come anywhere near it. Wrap a darkness about it, and in the centre of that darkness let his sense of ownership-in-Time lie silent, uninspected, and operative.

The sense of ownership in general is always to be encouraged. The humans are always putting up claims to ownership which sound equally funny in Heaven and in Hell, and we must keep them doing so. Much of the modern resistance to chastity comes from men's belief that they "own" their bodies—those vast and perilous estates, pulsating with the energy that made the worlds, in which they find themselves without their consent and from which they are ejected at the pleasure of Another! It is as if a royal child whom his father has placed, for love's sake, in titular command of some great province, under the real rule of wise counsellors, should come to fancy he really owns the cities, the forests, and the corn, in the same way as he owns the bricks on the nursery floor.

We produce this sense of ownership not only by pride but by confusion. We teach them not to notice the different senses of the possessive pronoun—the finely graded differences that run from "my boots" through "my dog," "my servant," "my wife," "my father," "my master," and "my country," to "my God." They can be taught to reduce all these senses to that of "my boots," the "my" of ownership. Even in the nursery a child can be taught to mean by "my Teddy bear" *not* the old imagined recipient of affection to whom it stands in a special relation (for that is what the Enemy will teach them to mean if we are not careful), but "the bear I can pull to pieces if I like." And at the other end of the scale, we have taught men to say "my God" in a sense not really very different from "my boots," meaning "The God on whom I have a claim for my distinguished services and whom I exploit from the pulpit—the God I have done a corner in."

And all the time the joke is that the word "mine" in its fully possessive sense cannot be uttered by a human being about anything. In the long run either Our Father or the Enemy will say "mine" of each thing that exists, and specially of each man. They will find out in the end, never fear, to whom their time, their souls, and their bodies really belong—certainly not to *them*, whatever happens. At present the Enemy says "mine" of everything on the pedantic, legalistic ground that He made it. Our Father hopes in the end to say "mine" of all things on the more realistic and dynamic ground of conquest.

Your affectionate uncle

SCREWTAPE

XXII

love theme

*M*y dear Wormwood,

So! Your man is in love—and in the worst kind he could possibly have fallen into—and with a girl who does not even appear in the report you sent me. You may be interested to learn that the little misunderstanding with the Secret Police which you tried to raise about some unguarded expressions in one of my letters has been tided over. If you were reckoning on that to secure my good offices, you will find yourself mistaken. You shall pay for that as well as for your other blunders. Meanwhile I enclose a little booklet, just issued, on the new House of Correction for Incompetent Tempters. It is profusely illustrated, and you will not find a dull page in it.

I have looked up this girl's dossier and am horrified at what I find. Not only a Christian but such a Christian—a vile, sneaking, simpering, demure, monosyllabic, mouselike, watery, insignificant, virginal, bread-and-butter miss! The little brute! She makes me vomit. She stinks and scalds through the very pages of the dossier. It drives me mad, the way the world has worsened. We'd have had her to the arena in the old days. That's what her sort is made for. Not that she'd do much good there, either. A two-faced little cheat (I know the sort) who looks as if she'd faint at the sight of blood, and then dies with a smile. A cheat every way. Looks as if butter wouldn't melt in her mouth, and yet has a satirical wit. The sort of creature who'd find *ME* funny! Filthy, insipid little prude— and yet ready to fall into this booby's arms like any other breeding animal. Why doesn't the Enemy blast her for it, if He's so moonstruck by virginity—instead of looking on there, grinning?

He's a hedonist at heart. All those fasts and vigils and stakes and crosses are only a façade. Or only like foam on the seashore. Out at sea, out in His sea, there is pleasure, and more pleasure. He makes no secret of it; at His right hand are "pleasures for evermore." Ugh! I don't think He has the least inkling of that high and austere mystery to which we rise in the Miserific Vision. He's vulgar, Wormwood. He has a bourgeois mind. He has filled His world full of pleasures. There are things for humans to do all day long without His minding in the least—sleeping, washing, eating, drinking, making love, playing, praying, working. Everything has to be *twisted* before it's any use to us. We fight under cruel disadvantages. Nothing is naturally on our side. (Not that that excuses *you*. I'll settle with you presently. You have always hated me and been insolent when you dared.)

Then, of course, he gets to know this woman's family and whole circle. Could you not see that the very house she lives in is one that he ought never to have entered? The whole place reeks of that deadly odour. The very gardener, though he has been there only five years, is beginning to acquire it. Even guests, after a weekend visit, carry some of the smell away with them. The dog and the cat are tainted with it. And a house full of the impenetrable mystery. We are certain (it is a matter of first principles) that each member of the family must in some way be making capital out of the others—but we can't find out how. They guard as jealously as the Enemy Himself the secret of what really lies behind this pretence of disinterested love. The whole house and garden is one vast obscenity. It bears a sickening resemblance to the description one human writer made of Heaven: "the regions where there is only life and therefore all that is not music is silence."

Music and silence—how I detest them both! How thankful we should be that ever since our Father entered Hell—though longer ago than humans, reckoning in light years, could express—no square inch of infernal space and no moment of infernal time has been surrendered to either of those abominable forces, but all has been occupied by Noise—Noise, the grand dynamism, the audible expression of all that is exultant, ruthless, and virile—Noise which alone defends us from silly qualms, despairing scruples, and impossible desires. We will make the whole universe a noise in the end. We have already made great strides in this direction as regards the Earth. The melodies and silences of Heaven will be shouted down in the end. But I admit we are not yet loud enough, or anything like it. Research is in progress. Meanwhile *you*, disgusting little—

[Here the MS. breaks off and is resumed in a different hand.]

he turned into a centipede b/c of anger

In the heat of composition I find that I have inadvertently allowed myself to assume the form of a large centipede. I am accordingly dictating the rest to my secretary. Now that the transformation is complete, I recognise it as a periodical phenomenon. Some rumour of it has reached the humans, and a distorted account of it appears in the poet Milton, with the ridiculous addition that such changes of shape are a "punishment" imposed on us by the Enemy. A more modern writer—someone with a name like Pshaw—has, however, grasped the truth. Transformation proceeds from within, and is a glorious manifestation of that Life Force which Our Father would worship if he worshipped anything but himself. In my present form I feel even more anxious to see you, to unite you to myself in an indissoluble embrace.

(Signed) TOADPIPE

For His Abysmal Sublimity Undersecretary
Screwtape, T.E., B.S., etc.

XXIII

*M*y dear Wormwood,

Through this girl and her disgusting family the patient is now getting to know more Christians every day, and very intelligent Christians too. For a long time it will be quite impossible to *remove* spirituality from his life. Very well, then; we must *corrupt* it. No doubt you have often practised transforming yourself into an angel of light as a parade-ground exercise. Now is the time to do it in the face of the Enemy. The World and the Flesh have failed us; a third Power remains. And success of this third kind is the most glorious of all. A spoiled saint, a Pharisee, an inquisitor, or a magician, makes better sport in Hell than a mere common tyrant or debauchee.

Looking round your patient's new friends, I find that the best point of attack would be the border-line between theology and politics. Several of his new friends are very much alive to the social implications of their religion. That, in itself, is a bad thing; but good can be made out of it.

You will find that a good many Christian-political writers think that Christianity began going wrong, and departing from the doctrine of its Founder, at a very early stage. Now, this idea must be used by us to encourage once again the conception of a "historical Jesus" to be found by clearing away later "accretions and perversions" and then to be contrasted with the whole Christian tradition. In the last generation we promoted the construction of such a "historical Jesus" on liberal and humanitarian lines; we are now putting forward a new "historical Jesus" on Marxian, catastrophic, and revolutionary lines. The advantages of these constructions, which we intend to change every thirty years or so, are manifold. In the first place they all tend to direct men's devotion to something which does not exist, for each "historical Jesus" is unhistorical. The documents say what they say and cannot be added to; each new "historical Jesus" therefore has to be got out of them by suppression at one point and exaggeration at another, and by that sort of guessing (*brilliant* is the adjective we teach humans to apply to it) on which no one would risk ten shillings in ordinary life, but which is enough to produce a crop of new Napoleons, new Shakespeares, and new Swifts, in every publisher's autumn list. In the second place, all such constructions place the importance of their "historical Jesus" in some peculiar theory He is supposed to have promulgated. He has to be a "great man" in the modern sense of the word— one standing at the terminus of some centrifugal and unbalanced line of thought—a crank vending a panacea. We thus distract men's minds from

Who He is, and what He did. We first make Him solely a teacher, and then conceal the very substantial agreement between His teachings and those of all other great moral teachers. For humans must not be allowed to notice that all great moralists are sent by the Enemy, not to inform men, but to remind them, to restate the primeval moral platitudes against our continual concealment of them. We make the Sophists: He raises up a Socrates to answer them. Our third aim is, by these constructions, to destroy the devotional life. For the real presence of the Enemy, otherwise experienced by men in prayer and sacrament, we substitute a merely probable, remote, shadowy, and uncouth figure, one who spoke a strange language and died a long time ago. Such an object cannot in fact be worshipped. Instead of the Creator adored by its creature, you soon have merely a leader acclaimed by a partisan, and finally a distinguished character approved by a judicious historian. And fourthly, besides being unhistorical in the Jesus it depicts, religion of this kind is false to history in another sense. No nation, and few individuals, are really brought into the Enemy's camp by the historical study of the biography of Jesus, simply as biography. Indeed, materials for a full biography have been withheld from men. The earliest converts were converted by a single historical fact (the Resurrection) and a single theological doctrine (the Redemption) operating on a sense of sin which they already had—and sin, not against some new fancy-dress law produced as a novelty by a "great man," but against the old, platitudinous, universal moral law which they had been taught by their nurses and mothers. The "Gospels" come later, and were written, not to make Christians, but to edify Christians already made.

The "historical Jesus," then, however dangerous he may seem to be to us at some particular point, is always to be encouraged. About the general connection between Christianity and politics, our position is more delicate. Certainly we do not want men to allow their Christianity to flow over into their political life, for the establishment of anything like a really just society would be a major disaster. On the other hand we do want, and want very much, to make men treat Christianity as a means; preferably, of course, as a means to their own advancement, but, failing that, as a means to anything—even to social justice. The thing to do is to get a man at first to value social justice as a thing which the Enemy demands, and then work him on to the stage at which he values Christianity because it may produce social justice. For the Enemy will not be used as a convenience. Men or nations who think they can revive the Faith in order to make a good society might just as well think they can use the stairs of Heaven as a short cut to the nearest chemist's shop. Fortunately it is quite easy to coax humans round this little corner. Only today I have found a passage in a Christian writer where he recommends his own version of Christianity on the ground that "only such a faith can outlast the death of

old cultures and the birth of new civilisations."
You see the little rift? "Believe this, not because it
is true, but for some other reason." That's the
game.

Your affectionate uncle

SCREWTAPE

XXIV

*M*y dear Wormwood,

I have been in correspondence with Slumtrimpet who is in charge of your patient's young woman, and begin to see the chink in her armour. It is an unobtrusive little vice which she shares with nearly all women who have grown up in an intelligent circle united by a clearly defined belief; and it consists in a quite untroubled assumption that the outsiders who do not share this belief are really too stupid and ridiculous. The males, who habitually meet these outsiders, do not feel that way; their confidence, if they are confident, is of a different kind. Hers, which she supposes to be due to Faith, is in reality largely due to the mere colour she has taken from her surroundings. It is not, in fact, very different from the conviction she would have felt at the age of ten that the kind of fish knives used in her father's house were the proper or normal or "real" kind, while those of the neighbouring families were "not real fish knives" at all. Now the element of ignorance and naïveté in all this is so large, and the element of spiritual pride so small, that it gives us little hope of the girl herself. But have you thought of how it can be made to influence your own patient?

It is always the novice who exaggerates. The man who has risen in society is overrefined; the young scholar is pedantic. In this new circle your patient is a novice. He is there daily, meeting Christian life of a quality he never before imagined and seeing it all through an enchanted glass because he is in love. He is anxious (indeed the Enemy commands him) to imitate this quality. Can you get him to imitate this *defect* in his mistress and to exaggerate it until what was venial in her becomes in him the strongest and most beautiful of the vices—Spiritual Pride?

The conditions seem ideally favourable. The new circle in which he finds himself is one of which he is tempted to be proud for many reasons other than its Christianity. It is a better educated, more intelligent, more agreeable society than any he has yet encountered. He is also under some degree of illusion as to his own place in it. Under the influence of "love" he may still think himself unworthy of the girl, but he is rapidly ceasing to think himself unworthy of the others. He has no notion how much in him is forgiven because they are charitable and made the best of because he is now one of the family. He does not dream how much of his conversation, how many of his opinions, are recognised by them all as mere echoes of their own. Still less does he suspect how much of the delight he takes in these people is due to the erotic enchantment which the girl, for him, spreads over all her surroundings. He thinks that he likes their talk and way of life because of some congruity between their spiritual state and his, when in fact they are so far beyond him that if he were not in love he would be merely puzzled and repelled by much which he now accepts. He is like a dog which should imagine it understood firearms because its hunting instinct and love for its master enable it to enjoy a day's shooting!

Here is your chance. While the Enemy, by means of sexual love and of some very agreeable people far advanced in His service, is drawing the young barbarian up to levels he could never otherwise have reached, you must make him feel that he is finding his *own* level—that these people are "his sort" and that, coming among them, he has come home. When he turns from them to other society he will find it dull; partly because almost any society within his reach is, in fact, much less entertaining, but still more because he will miss the enchantment of the young woman. You must teach him to mistake this contrast between the circle that delights and the circle that bores him for the contrast between Christians and unbelievers. He must be made to feel (he'd better not put it into words) "how different we Christians are"; and by "we Christians" he must really, but unknowingly, mean "my set"; and by "my set" he must mean not "the people who, in their charity and humility, have accepted me," but "the people with whom I associate by right."

Success here depends on confusing him. If you

try to make him explicitly and professedly proud of being a Christian, you will probably fail; the Enemy's warnings are too well known. If, on the other hand, you let the idea of "we Christians" drop out altogether and merely make him complacent about "his set," you will produce not true spiritual pride but mere social vanity which, by comparison, is a trumpery, puny little sin. What you want is to keep a sly self-congratulation mixing with all his thoughts and never allow him to raise the question "What, precisely, am I congratulating myself about?" The idea of belonging to an inner ring, of being in a secret, is very sweet to him. Play on that nerve. Teach him, using the influence of this girl when she is silliest, to adopt an air of *amusement* at the things the unbelievers say. Some theories which he may meet in modern Christian circles may here prove helpful; theories, I mean, that place the hope of society in some inner ring of "clerks," some trained minority of theocrats. It is no affair of yours whether those theories are true or false; the great thing is to make Christianity a mystery religion in which he feels himself one of the initiates.

Pray do not fill your letters with rubbish about this European War. Its final issue is, no doubt, important, but that is a matter for the High Command. I am not in the least interested in knowing how many people in England have been killed by bombs. In what state of mind they died, I can learn from the office at this end. That they were going to die sometime I knew already. Please keep your mind on your work.

Your affectionate uncle

SCREWTAPE

XXV

*M*y dear Wormwood,

The real trouble about the set your patient is living in is that it is *merely* Christian. They all have individual interests, of course, but the bond remains mere Christianity. What we want, if men become Christians at all, is to keep them in the state of mind I call "Christianity And." You know—Christianity and the Crisis, Christianity and the New Psychology, Christianity and the New Order, Christianity and Faith Healing, Christianity and Psychical Research, Christianity and Vegetarianism, Christianity and Spelling Reform. If they must be Christians, let them at least be Christians with a difference. Substitute for the faith itself some Fashion with a Christian colouring. Work on their horror of the Same Old Thing.

The horror of the Same Old Thing is one of the most valuable passions we have produced in the human heart—an endless source of heresies in religion, folly in counsel, infidelity in marriage, and inconstancy in friendship. The humans live in time, and experience reality successively. To experience much of it, therefore, they must experience many different things; in other words, they must experience change. And since they need change, the Enemy (being a hedonist at heart) has made change pleasurable to them, just as He has made eating pleasurable. But since He does not wish them to make change, any more than eating, an end in itself, He has balanced the love of change in them by a love of permanence. He has contrived to gratify both tastes together in the very world He has made, by that union of change and permanence which we call Rhythm. He gives them the seasons, each season different yet every year the same, so that spring is always felt as a novelty yet always as the recurrence of an immemorial theme. He gives them in His Church a spiritual year; they change from a fast to a feast, but it is the same feast as before.

Now just as we pick out and exaggerate the pleasure of eating to produce gluttony, so we pick out this natural pleasantness of change and twist it into a demand for absolute novelty. This demand is entirely our workmanship. If we neglect our duty, men will be not only contented but transported by the mixed novelty and familiarity of snowdrops *this* January, sunrise *this* morning, plum pudding *this* Christmas. Children, until we have taught them better, will be perfectly happy with a seasonal round of games in which conkers succeed hopscotch as regularly as autumn follows summer. Only by our incessant efforts is the demand for infinite, or unrhythmical, change kept up.

This demand is valuable in various ways. In the

first place it diminishes pleasure while increasing desire. The pleasure of novelty is by its very nature more subject than any other to the law of diminishing returns. And continued novelty costs money, so that the desire for it spells avarice or unhappiness or both. And again, the more rapacious this desire, the sooner it must eat up all the innocent sources of pleasure and pass on to those the Enemy forbids. Thus by inflaming the horror of the Same Old Thing, we have recently made the Arts, for example, less dangerous to us than, perhaps, they have ever been, "lowbrow" and "highbrow" artists alike being now daily drawn into fresh, and still fresh, excesses of lasciviousness, unreason, cruelty, and pride. Finally, the desire for novelty is indispensable if we are to produce Fashions or Vogues.

The use of Fashions in thought is to distract the attention of men from their real dangers. We direct the fashionable outcry of each generation against those vices of which it is least in danger and fix its approval on the virtue nearest to that vice which we are trying to make endemic. The game is to have them all running about with fire extinguishers whenever there is a flood, and all crowding to that side of the boat which is already nearly gunwale under. Thus we make it fashionable to expose the dangers of enthusiasm at the very moment when they are all really becoming worldly and lukewarm; a century later, when we are really making them all Byronic and drunk with emotion, the fashionable outcry is directed against the dangers of the mere "understanding."

Cruel ages are put on their guard against Sentimentality, feckless and idle ones against Respectability, lecherous ones against Puritanism; and whenever all men are really hastening to be slaves or tyrants we make Liberalism the prime bogey.

But the greatest triumph of all is to elevate this horror of the Same Old Thing into a philosophy so that nonsense in the intellect may reinforce corruption in the will. It is here that the general Evolutionary or Historical character of modern European thought (partly our work) comes in so usefully. The Enemy loves platitudes. Of a proposed course of action He wants men, so far as I can see, to ask very simple questions: Is it righteous? Is it prudent? Is it possible? Now if we can keep men asking: "Is it in accordance with the general movement of our time? Is it progressive or reactionary? Is this the way that History is going?" they will neglect the relevant questions. And the questions they do ask are, of course, unanswerable; for they do not know the future, and what the future will be depends very largely on just those choices which they now invoke the future to help them to make. As a result, while their minds are buzzing in this vacuum, we have the better chance to slip in and bend them to the action *we* have decided on. And great work has already been done. Once they knew that some changes were for the better, and others for the worse, and others again indifferent. We have largely removed this knowledge. For the descriptive adjective "unchanged" we have substituted the emotional adjective "stagnant." We have trained them to think of the future as a promised land which favoured heroes attain—not as something which everyone reaches at the rate of sixty minutes an hour, whatever he does, whoever he is.

Your affectionate uncle

SCREWTAPE

XXVI

*M*y dear Wormwood,

Yes; courtship is the time for sowing those seeds which will grow up ten years later into domestic hatred. The enchantment of unsatisfied desire produces results which the humans can be made to mistake for the results of charity. Avail yourself of the ambiguity in the word "Love": let them think they have solved by Love problems they have in fact only waived or postponed under the influence of the enchantment. While it lasts you have your chance to foment the problems in secret and render them chronic.

The grand problem is that of "Unselfishness." Note, once again, the admirable work of our Philological Arm in substituting the negative unselfishness for the Enemy's positive Charity. Thanks to this you can, from the very outset, teach a man to surrender benefits not that others may be happy in having them but that he may be unselfish in forgoing them. That is a great point gained. Another great help, where the parties concerned are male and female, is the divergence of view about Unselfishness which we have built up between the sexes. A woman means by Unselfishness chiefly taking trouble for others; a man means not giving trouble to others. As a result, a woman who is quite far gone in the Enemy's service will make a nuisance of herself on a larger scale than any man except those whom Our Father has dominated completely; and, conversely, a man will live long in the Enemy's camp before he undertakes as much spontaneous work to please others as a quite ordinary woman may do every day. Thus while the woman thinks of doing good offices and the man of respecting other people's rights, each sex, without any obvious unreason, can and does regard the other as radically selfish.

On top of these confusions you can now introduce a few more. The erotic enchantment produces a mutual complaisance in which each is *really* pleased to give in to the wishes of the other. They also know that the Enemy demands of them a degree of charity which, if attained, would result in similar actions. You must make them establish as a Law for their whole married life that degree of mutual self-sacrifice which is at present sprouting naturally out of the enchantment but which, when the enchantment dies away, they will not have charity enough to enable them to perform. They will not see the trap, since they are under the double blindness of mistaking sexual excitement for charity and of thinking that the excitement will last.

When once a sort of official, legal, or nominal Unselfishness has been established as a rule—a rule for the keeping of which their emotional resources have died away and their spiritual resources have not yet grown—the most delightful results follow. In discussing any joint action, it becomes obligatory that A should argue in favour of B's supposed wishes and against his own, while B does the opposite. It is often impossible to find out either party's real wishes; with luck, they end by doing something that neither wants, while each feels a glow of self-righteousness and harbours a secret claim to preferential treatment for the unselfishness shown and a secret grudge against the other for the ease with which the sacrifice has been accepted. Later on, you can venture on what may be called the Generous Conflict Illusion. This game is best played with more than two players, in a family with grown-up children, for example. Something quite trivial, like having tea in the garden, is proposed. One member takes care to make it quite clear (though not in so many words) that he would rather not but is, of course, prepared to do so out of "Unselfishness." The others instantly withdraw their proposal, ostensibly through their "Unselfishness," but really because they don't want to be used as a sort of lay figure on which the first speaker practices petty altruisms. But he is not going to be done out of his debauch of Unselfishness either. He insists on doing "what the others want." They insist on doing what he wants. Passions are roused. Soon someone is saying, "Very well, then, I won't have any tea at all!" and a real quarrel ensues with bitter resentment on both sides. You see how it is done? If each side had been frankly contending for its own real wish, they would all have kept within the bounds of reason and courtesy; but just because the contention is reversed and each side is fighting the other side's battle, all the bitterness which really flows from thwarted self-righteousness and obstinacy and from the accumulated grudges of the last ten years is concealed from them by the nominal or official "Unselfishness" of what they are doing or, at least, held to be excused by it. Each side is, indeed, quite alive to the cheap quality of the adversary's Unselfishness and of the false position into which he is trying to force them; but each manages to feel blameless and ill-used itself, with no more dishonesty than comes natural to a human.

A sensible human once said, "If people knew how much ill-feeling Unselfishness occasions, it would not be so often recommended from the pulpit"; and again, "She's the sort of woman who lives for others—you can always tell the others by their hunted expression." All this can be begun even in the period of courtship. A little *real* selfishness on your patient's part is often of less value in the long run, for securing his soul, than the first beginnings of that elaborate and self-conscious unselfishness which may one day blossom into the sort of thing I have described. Some degree of mutual falseness, some surprise that the girl does not always notice just how Unselfish he is being, can be smuggled in already. Cherish these things, and, above all, don't let the young fools notice them. If they notice them they will be on the road to discovering that "love" is not enough, that charity is needed and not yet achieved and that no external law can supply its place. I wish Slumtrimpet could do something about undermining that young woman's sense of the ridiculous.

Your affectionate uncle

SCREWTAPE

XXVII

*M*y dear Wormwood,

You seem to be doing very little good at present. The use of his "love" to distract his mind from the Enemy is, of course, obvious, but you reveal what poor use you are making of it when you say that the whole question of distraction and the wandering mind has now become one of the chief subjects of his prayers. That means you have largely failed. When this, or any other distraction, crosses his mind you ought to encourage him to thrust it away by sheer will power and to try to continue the normal prayer as if nothing had happened; once he accepts the distraction as his present problem and lays *that* before the Enemy and makes it the main theme of his prayers and his endeavours, then, so far from doing good, you have done harm. Anything, even a sin, which has the total effect of moving him close up to the Enemy, makes against us in the long run.

A promising line is the following: Now that he is in love, a new idea of *earthly* happiness has arisen in his mind; and hence a new urgency in his purely petitionary prayers—about this war and other such matters. Now is the time for raising intellectual difficulties about prayer of that sort. False spirituality is always to be encouraged. On the seemingly pious ground that "praise and communion with God is the true prayer," humans can often be lured into direct disobedience to the Enemy Who (in His usual flat, commonplace, uninteresting way) has definitely told them to pray for their daily bread and the recovery of their sick. You will, of course, conceal from him the fact that the prayer for daily bread, interpreted in a "spiritual sense," is really just as crudely petitionary as it is in any other sense.

But since your patient has contracted the terrible habit of obedience, he will probably continue such "crude" prayers whatever you do. But you can worry him with the haunting suspicion that the practice is absurd and can have no objective result. Don't forget to use the "Heads I win, tails you lose" argument. If the thing he prays for doesn't happen, then that is one more proof that petitionary prayers don't work; if it does happen, he will, of course, be able to see some of the physical causes which led up to it, and "therefore it would have happened anyway," and thus a granted prayer becomes just as good a proof as a denied one that prayers are ineffective.

You, being a spirit, will find it difficult to understand how he gets into this confusion. But you must remember that he takes Time for an ultimate reality. He supposes that the Enemy, like himself, sees some things as present, remembers others as past, and anticipates others as future;

or even if he believes that the Enemy does not see things that way, yet, in his heart of hearts, he regards this as a peculiarity of the Enemy's mode of perception—he doesn't really think (though he would say he did) that things as the Enemy sees them are things as they are! If you tried to explain to him that men's prayers today are one of the innumerable coordinates with which the Enemy harmonises the weather of tomorrow, he would reply that then the Enemy always knew men were going to make those prayers and, if so, they did not pray freely but were predestined to do so. And he would add that the weather on a given day can be traced back through its causes to the original creation of matter itself—so that the whole thing, both on the human and on the material side, is given "from the word go." What he ought to say, of course, is obvious to us: that the problem of adapting the particular weather to the particular prayers is merely the appearance, at two points in his temporal mode of perception, of the total problem of adapting the whole spiritual universe to the whole corporeal universe; that creation in its entirety operates at every point of space and time, or rather that their kind of consciousness forces them to encounter the whole, self-consistent creative act as a series of successive events. *Why* that creative act leaves room for their free will is the problem of problems, the secret behind the Enemy's nonsense about "Love." *How* it does so is no problem at all; for the enemy does not *foresee* the humans making their free contributions in a future, but *sees* them doing so in His unbounded

Now. And obviously to watch a man doing something is not to make him do it.

It may be replied that some meddlesome human writers, notably Boethius, have let this secret out. But in the intellectual climate which we have at last succeeded in producing throughout western Europe, you needn't bother about that. Only the learned read old books, and we have now so dealt with the learned that they are of all men the least likely to acquire wisdom by doing so. We have done this by inculcating the Historical Point of View. The Historical Point of View, put briefly, means that when a learned man is presented with any statement in an ancient author, the one question he never asks is whether it is true. He asks who influenced the ancient writer, and how far the statement is consistent with what he said in other books, and what phase in the writer's development, or in the general history of thought, it illustrates, and how it affected later writers, and how often it has been misunderstood (specially by the learned man's own colleagues) and what the general course of criticism on it has been for the last ten years, and what is the "present state of the question." To regard the ancient writer as a possible source of knowledge—to anticipate that what he said could possibly modify your thoughts or your behaviour—this would be rejected as unutterably simple-minded. And since we cannot deceive the whole human race all the time, it is most important thus to cut every generation off from all others; for where learning makes a free commerce between the ages there is always the danger that the characteristic errors of one may be corrected by the characteristic truths of another. But thanks be to Our Father and the Historical Point of View, great scholars are now as little nourished by the past as the most ignorant mechanic who holds that "history is bunk."

Your affectionate uncle

SCREWTAPE

XXVIII

*M*y dear Wormwood,

When I told you not to fill your letters with rubbish about the war, I meant, of course, that I did not want to have your rather infantile rhapsodies about the death of men and the destruction of cities. In so far as the war really concerns the spiritual state of the patient, I naturally want full reports. And on this aspect you seem singularly obtuse. Thus you tell me with glee that there is reason to expect heavy air raids on the town where the creature lives. This is a crying example of something I have complained about already—your readiness to forget the main point in your immediate enjoyment of human suffering. Do you not know that bombs kill men? Or do you not realise that the patient's death, at this moment, is precisely what we want to avoid? He has escaped the worldly friends with whom you tried to entangle him; he has "fallen in love" with a very Christian woman and is temporarily immune from your attacks on his chastity; and the various methods of corrupting his spiritual life which we have been trying are so far unsuccessful. At the present moment, as the full impact of the war draws nearer and his worldly hopes take a proportionately lower place in his mind, full of his defence work, full of the girl, forced to attend to his neighbours more than he has ever done before and liking it more than he expected, "taken out of himself," as the humans say, and daily increasing in conscious dependence on the Enemy, he will almost certainly be lost to us if he is killed tonight. This is so obvious that I am ashamed to write it. I sometimes wonder if you young fiends are not kept out on temptation duty too long at a time—if you are not in some danger of becoming infected by the sentiments and values of the humans among whom you work. They, of course, do tend to regard death as the prime evil, and survival as the greatest good. But that is because we have taught them to do so. Do not let us be infected by our own propaganda. I know it seems strange that your chief aim at the moment should be the very same thing for which the patient's lover and his mother are praying—namely, his bodily safety. But so it is; you should be guarding him like the apple of your eye. If he dies now, you lose him. If he survives the war, there is always hope. The Enemy has guarded him from you through the first great wave of temptations. But, if only he can be kept alive, you have time itself for your ally. The long, dull, monotonous years of middle-aged prosperity or middle-aged adversity are excellent campaigning weather. You see, it is so hard for these creatures to *persevere*. The routine of adversity, the gradual decay of youthful loves and youthful hopes, the quiet despair (hardly felt as pain) of ever overcoming the chronic temptations with which we have again and again defeated them, the drabness which we create in their lives, and the inarticulate resentment with which we teach them to respond to it—all this provides admirable opportunities of wearing out a soul by attrition. If, on the other hand, the middle years prove prosperous, our position is even stronger. Prosperity knits a man to the World. He feels that he is "finding his place in it," while really it is finding its place in him. His increasing reputation, his widening circle of acquaintances, his sense of importance, the growing pressure of absorbing and agreeable work, build up in him a sense of being really at home on Earth, which is just what we want. You will notice that the young are generally less unwilling to die than the middle-aged and the old.

The truth is that the Enemy, having oddly destined these mere animals to life in His own eternal world, has guarded them pretty effectively from the danger of feeling at home anywhere else. That is why we must often wish long life to our patients; seventy years is not a day too much for the difficult task of unravelling their souls from Heaven and building up a firm attachment to the Earth. While they are young we find them always shooting off at a tangent. Even if we contrive to keep them ignorant of explicit religion, the incalculable winds of fantasy and music and poetry—the mere face of a girl, the song of a bird, or the sight of a horizon—are always blowing our whole structure away. They *will* not apply themselves steadily to worldly advancement, prudent connections, and the policy of safety first. So inveterate is their appetite for Heaven, that our best method, at this stage, of attaching them to Earth is to make them believe that Earth can be turned into Heaven at some future date by politics or eugenics or "science" or psychology or what not. Real worldliness is a work of time—assisted, of course, by pride, for we teach them to describe the creeping death as Good Sense or Maturity or Experience. *Experience*, in the peculiar sense we teach them to give it, is, by the bye, a most useful word. A great human philosopher nearly let our secret out when he said that where Virtue is concerned "Experience is the mother of illusion"; but thanks to a change in Fashion, and also, of course, to the Historical Point of View, we have largely rendered his book innocuous.

How valuable time is to us may be gauged by the fact that the Enemy allows us so little of it. The majority of the human race dies in infancy; of the survivors, a good many die in youth. It is obvious that to Him human birth is important chiefly as the qualification for human death, and death solely as the gate to that other kind of life. We are allowed to work only on a selected minority of the race, for what humans call a "normal life" is the exception. Apparently He wants some—but only a very few—of the human animals with which He is peopling Heaven to have had the experience of resisting us through an earthly life of sixty or seventy years. Well, there is our opportunity. The smaller it is, the better we must use it. Whatever you do, keep your patient as safe as you possibly can.

> Your affectionate uncle
>> SCREWTAPE

XXIX

*M*y dear Wormwood,

Now that it is certain the German humans will bombard your patient's town and that his duties will keep him in the thick of the danger, we must consider our policy. Are we to aim at cowardice—or at courage, with consequent pride—or at hatred of the Germans?

Well, I am afraid it is no good trying to make him brave. Our Research Department has not yet discovered (though success is hourly expected) how to produce *any* virtue. This is a serious handicap. To be greatly and effectively wicked a man needs some virtue. What would Attila have been without his courage, or Shylock without self-denial as regards the flesh? But as we cannot supply these qualities ourselves, we can only use them as supplied by the Enemy—and this means leaving Him a kind of foothold in those men whom, otherwise, we have made most securely our own. A very unsatisfactory arrangement, but, I trust, we shall one day learn to do better.

Hatred we can manage. The tension of human nerves during noise, danger, and fatigue, makes them prone to any violent emotion, and it is only a question of guiding this susceptibility into the right channels. If conscience resists, muddle him. Let him say that he feels hatred not on his own behalf but on that of the women and children, and that a Christian is told to forgive his own, not other people's enemies. In other words let him consider himself sufficiently identified with the women and children to feel hatred on their behalf, but *not* sufficiently identified to regard their enemies as his own and therefore proper objects of forgiveness.

But hatred is best combined with Fear. Cowardice, alone of all the vices, is purely painful— horrible to anticipate, horrible to feel, horrible to remember; Hatred has its pleasures. It is therefore often the *compensation* by which a frightened man reimburses himself for the miseries of Fear. The more he fears, the more he will hate. And Hatred is also a great anodyne for shame. To make a deep wound in his charity, you should therefore first defeat his courage.

Now, this is a ticklish business. We have made men proud of most vices, but not of cowardice. Whenever we have almost succeeded in doing so, the Enemy permits a war or an earthquake or some other calamity, and at once courage becomes so obviously lovely and important even in human eyes that all our work is undone, and there is still at least one vice of which they feel genuine shame. The danger of inducing cowardice in our patients, therefore, is lest we produce real self-knowledge and self-loathing, with consequent repentance and humility. And in fact, in the last war, thousands of humans, by discovering their own cowardice, discovered the whole moral world for the first time. In peace we can make many of them ignore good and evil entirely; in danger, the issue is forced upon them in a guise to which even we cannot blind them. There is here a cruel dilemma before us. If we promoted justice and charity among men, we should be playing directly into the Enemy's hands; but if we guide them to the opposite behaviour, this sooner or later produces (for He permits it to produce) a war or a revolution, and the undisguisable issue of cowardice or courage awakes thousands of men from moral stupor.

This, indeed, is probably one of the Enemy's motives for creating a dangerous world—a world in which moral issues really come to the point. He sees as well as you do that courage is not simply one of the virtues, but the form of every virtue at the testing point, which means, at the point of highest reality. A chastity or honesty or mercy which yields to danger will be chaste or honest or merciful only on conditions. Pilate was merciful till it became risky.

It is therefore possible to lose as much as we gain by making your man a coward; he may learn too much about himself! There is, of course, always the chance, not of chloroforming the shame, but of aggravating it and producing Despair. This would be a great triumph. It would show that he had believed in, and accepted, the Enemy's forgiveness of his other sins only because he himself did not fully feel their sinfulness—that in respect of the one vice which he really understands in its full depth of dishonour he cannot seek, nor credit, the Mercy. But I fear you have already let him get too far in the Enemy's school, and he knows that Despair is a greater sin than any of the sins which provoke it.

As to the actual technique of temptations to cowardice, not much need be said. The main point is that precautions have a tendency to increase fear. The precautions publicly enjoined on your patient, however, soon become a matter of routine, and this effect disappears. What you must do is to keep running in his mind (side by side with the conscious intention of doing his duty) the vague idea of all sorts of things he can do or not do, *inside* the framework of the duty, which seem to make him a little safer. Get his mind off the simple rule ("I've got to stay here and do so-and-so") into a series of imaginary life lines ("If A happened—though I very much hope it won't—I could do B—and if the worst came to the worst, I could always do C"). Superstitions, if not recognised as such, can be awakened. The point is to keep him feeling that he has *something,* other than the Enemy and courage the Enemy supplies, *to fall back on,* so that what was intended to be a total commitment to duty becomes honeycombed all through with little unconscious reservations. By building up a series of imaginary expedients to prevent "the worst coming to the worst," you may produce, at that level of his will which he is not aware of, a determination that the worst *shall not* come to the worst. Then, at the moment of real terror, rush it out into his nerves and muscles and you may get the fatal act done before he knows what you're about. For remember: the *act* of cowardice is all that matters; the emotion of fear is, in itself, no sin and, though we enjoy it, does us no good.

Your affectionate uncle

SCREWTAPE

XXX

*M*y dear Wormwood,

I sometimes wonder whether you think you have been sent into the world for your own amusement. I gather, not from your miserably inadequate report but from that of the Infernal Police, that the patient's behaviour during the first raid has been the worst possible. He has been very frightened and thinks himself a great coward and therefore feels no pride; but he has done everything his duty demanded and perhaps a bit more. Against this disaster all you can produce on the credit side is a burst of ill temper with a dog that tripped him up, some excessive cigarette smoking, and the forgetting of a prayer. What is the use of whining to me about your difficulties? If you are proceeding on the Enemy's idea of "justice" and suggesting that your opportunities and intentions should be taken into account, then I am not sure that a charge of heresy does not lie against you. At any rate, you will soon find that the justice of Hell is purely realistic, and concerned only with results. Bring us back food, or be food yourself.

The only constructive passage in your letter is where you say that you still expect good results from the patient's fatigue. That is well enough. But it won't fall into your hands. Fatigue *can* produce extreme gentleness, and quiet of mind, and even something like vision. If you have often seen men led by it into anger, malice and impatience, that is because those men have had efficient tempers. The paradoxical thing is that moderate fatigue is a better soil for peevishness than absolute exhaustion. This depends partly on physical causes, but partly on something else. It is not fatigue simply as such that produces the anger, but unexpected demands on a man already tired. Whatever men expect they soon come to think they have a right to: the sense of disappointment can, with very little skill on our part, be turned into a sense of injury. It is after men have given in to the irremediable, after they have despaired of relief and ceased to think even a half-hour ahead, that the dangers of humbled and gentle weariness begin. To produce the best results from the patient's fatigue, therefore, you must feed him with false hopes. Put into his mind plausible reasons for believing that the air raid will not be repeated. Keep him comforting himself with the thought of how much he will enjoy his bed next night. Exaggerate the weariness by making him think it will soon be over; for men usually feel that a strain could have been endured no longer at the very moment when it is ending, or when they think it is ending. In this, as in the problem of cowardice, the thing to avoid is the total commitment. Whatever he *says*, let his inner resolution be not to bear whatever comes to him, but to bear it "for a reasonable period"—and let the reasonable period be shorter than the trial is likely to last. It need not be *much* shorter; in attacks on patience, chastity, and fortitude, the fun is to make the man yield just when (had he but known it) relief was almost in sight.

I do not know whether he is likely to meet the girl under conditions of strain or not. If he does, make full use of the fact that up to a certain point, fatigue makes women talk more and men talk less. Much secret resentment, even between lovers, can be raised from this.

Probably the scenes he is now witnessing will not provide material for an *intellectual* attack on his faith—your previous failures have put that out of your power. But there is a sort of attack on the emotions which can still be tried. It turns on making him *feel*, when first he sees human remains plastered on a wall, that this is "what the world is *really* like" and that all his religion has been a fantasy. You will notice that we have got them completely fogged about the meaning of the word "real." They tell each other, of some great spiritual experience, "All that *really* happened was that you heard some music in a lighted building"; here "real" means the bare physical facts, separated from the other elements in the experience they actually had. On the other hand, they will also say, "It's all very well discussing that high dive as you sit here in an armchair, but wait till you get up there and see what it's *really* like":

here "real" is being used in the opposite sense to mean, not the physical facts (which they know already while discussing the matter in armchairs), but the emotional effect those facts will have on a human consciousness. Either application of the word could be defended; but our business is to keep the two going at once so that the emotional value of the word "real" can be placed now on one side of the account, now on the other, as it happens to suit us. The general rule which we have now pretty well established among them is that in all experiences which can make them happier or better only the physical facts are "real," while the spiritual elements are "subjective"; in all experiences which can discourage or corrupt them the spiritual elements are the main reality, and to ignore them is to be an escapist. Thus in birth the blood and pain are "real," the rejoicing a mere subjective point of view; in death, the terror and ugliness reveal what death "really means." The hatefulness of a hated person is "real"—in hatred you see men as they are, you are disillusioned; but the loveliness of a loved person is merely a subjective haze concealing a "real" core of sexual appetite or economic association. Wars and poverty are "really" horrible; peace and plenty are mere physical facts about which men happen to have certain sentiments. The creatures are always accusing one another of wanting "to eat the cake and have it"; but thanks to our labours they are more often in the predicament of paying for the cake and not eating it. Your patient, properly handled, will have no difficulty in regarding his emo-

at the sight of human entrails as a revelation
reality and his emotion at the sight of happy
children or fair weather as mere sentiment.

Your affectionate uncle

SCREWTAPE

XXXI

My dear, my very dear, Wormwood, my poppet, my pigsnie,

How mistakenly, now that all is lost, you come whimpering to ask me whether the terms of affection in which I address you meant nothing from the beginning. Far from it! Rest assured, my love for you and your love for me are as like as two peas. I have always desired you, as you (pitiful fool) desired me. The difference is that I am the stronger. I think they will give you to me now; or a bit of you. Love you? Why, yes. As dainty a morsel as ever I grew fat on.

You have let a soul slip through your fingers. The howl of sharpened famine for that loss reechoes at this moment through all the levels of the Kingdom of Noise down to the very Throne itself. It makes me mad to think of it. How well I know what happened at the instant when they snatched him from you! There was a sudden clearing of his eyes (was there not?) as he saw you for the first time, and recognised the part you had had in him and knew that you had it no longer. Just think (and let it be the beginning of your ty) what he felt at that moment; as if a scab had fallen from an old sore, as if he were emerging from a hideous, shell-like tetter, as if he shuffled off for good and all a defiled, wet, clinging garment. By Hell, it is misery enough to see them in their mortal days taking off dirtied and uncomfortable clothes and splashing in hot water and giving little grunts of pleasure—stretching their eased limbs. What, then, of this final stripping, this complete cleansing?

The more one thinks about it, the worse it becomes. He got through so easily! No gradual misgivings, no doctor's sentence, no nursing home, no operating theatre, no false hopes of life: sheer, instantaneous liberation. One moment it seemed to be all our world; the scream of bombs, the fall of houses, the stink and taste of high explosive on the lips and in the lungs, the feet burning with weariness, the heart cold with horrors, the brain reeling, the legs aching; next moment all this was gone, gone like a bad dream, never again to be of any account. Defeated, outmanœuvred fool! Did you mark how naturally—as if he'd been born for it—the Earth-born vermin entered the new life? How all his doubts became, in the twinkling of an eye, ridiculous? I know what the creature was saying to itself! "Yes. Of course. It always was like this. All horrors have followed the same course, getting worse and worse and forcing you into a kind of bottleneck till, at the very moment when you thought you must be crushed, behold! you were out of the narrows and all was suddenly well.

The extraction hurt more and more and then the tooth was out. The dream became a nightmare and then you woke. You die and die and then you are beyond death. How could I ever have doubted it?"

As he saw you, he also saw Them. I know how it was. You reeled back dizzy and blinded, more hurt by them than he had ever been by bombs. The degradation of it!—that this thing of earth and slime could stand upright and converse with spirits before whom you, a spirit, could only cower. Perhaps you had hoped that the awe and strangeness of it would dash his joy. But that is the cursed thing; the gods are strange to mortal eyes, and yet they are not strange. He had no faintest conception till that very hour of how they would look, and even doubted their existence. But when he saw them he knew that he had always known them and realised what part each one of them had played at many an hour in his life when he had supposed himself alone, so that now he could say to them, one by one, not "Who *are* you?" but "So it was *you* all the time." All that they were and said at this meeting woke memories. The dim consciousness of friends about him which had haunted his solitudes from infancy was now at last explained; that central music in every pure experience which had always just evaded memory was now at last recovered. Recognition made him free of their company almost before the limbs of his corpse became quiet. Only you were left outside.

He saw not only Them; he saw Him. This animal, this thing begotten in a bed, could look on

. What is blinding, suffocating fire to you is ⟋ cool light to him, is clarity itself, and wears the form of a Man. You would like, if you could, to interpret the patient's prostration in the Presence, his self-abhorrence and utter knowledge of his sins (yes, Wormwood, a clearer knowledge even than yours) on the analogy of your own choking and paralysing sensations when you encounter the deadly air that breathes from the heart of Heaven. But it's all nonsense. Pains he may still have to encounter, but they *embrace* those pains. They would not barter them for any earthly pleasure. All the delights of sense, or heart, or intellect, with which you could once have tempted him, even the delights of virtue itself, now seem to him in comparison but as the half-nauseous attractions of a raddled harlot would seem to a man who hears that his true beloved whom he has loved all his life and whom he had believed to be dead is alive and even now at his door. He is caught up into that world where pain and pleasure take on transfinite values and all our arithmetic is dismayed. Once more, the inexplicable meets us. Next to the curse of useless tempters like yourself the greatest curse upon us is the failure of our Intelligence Department. If only we could find out what He is really up to! Alas, alas, that knowledge, in itself so hateful and mawkish a thing, should yet be necessary for Power! Sometimes I am almost in despair. All that sustains me is the conviction that our Realism, our rejection (in the face of all temptations) of all silly nonsense

and claptrap, *must* win in the end. Meanwhile, I
have you to settle with. Most truly do I sign myself
Your increasingly and ravenously
affectionate uncle
SCREWTAPE

There's an epidemic with 27 million victims. And no visible symptoms.

It's an epidemic of people who can't read.

Believe it or not, 27 million Americans are functionally illiterate, about one adult in five.

The solution to this problem is you... when you join the fight against illiteracy. So call the Coalition for Literacy at toll-free **1-800-228-8813** and volunteer.

Volunteer Against Illiteracy. The only degree you need is a degree of caring.